ONE DISCIPLE AT A TIME

"The Church today requires an approach to ministry that is not new, but is renewed. Everett Fritz places you at Jesus's heart and empowers you to do the same for others. This book is a gift for all those who, like Jesus, want to change the world one person at a time!"

Chris Bartlett
Director of Leadership Formation
Ablaze Ministries

"This book is wonderful! *One Disciple at a Time* explains the ministry of one. By taking an interest in someone, caring about them, and—when appropriate—mentoring them, we can help lead that person to make Jesus their number-one love. This book will help believers to become disciples who, in turn, make more disciples just as Jesus commanded us to do."

Fr. Richard Gray
Pastor of Our Lady of Perpetual Help and Our Lady of Sorrows Parishes
Archdiocese of Baltimore

"Everett Fritz prompts us to ask, 'If my ministry was only focused on one person, what would it look like?' If we can't answer that question, are we actually doing ministry? Too often we're not: we're running programs. Programs are great tools, but if the program is about the program, we're missing the point. This book is a call to do ministry as Jesus did—focused on one: the lost sheep, the found coin, the intimate conversation. Everything else we build needs to flow from that."

Chris Stefanick
Founder and president of Real Life Catholic

ONE DISCIPLE AT A TIME

How to LEAD OTHERS to DYNAMIC, ENGAGED, LIFE-CHANGING FAITH

EVERETT FRITZ

Founded in 1865, Ave Maria Press is a ministry of the United States Province of Holy Cross.

www.avemariapress.com

Paperback: ISBN-13 978-1-64680-143-5

E-book: ISBN-13 978-1-64680-144-2

Cover and text design by Christopher D. Tobin.

Printed and bound in the United States of America.

Library of Congress Cataloging-in-Publication Data
Names: Fritz, Everett, author.
Title: One disciple at a time : how to lead others to dynamic, engaged, life-changing faith / Everett Fritz.
Description: Notre Dame, Indiana : Ave Maria Press, [2022] | Includes bibliographical references. | Summary: "In this book Everett Fritz, popular author, ministry coach, and founder of Andrew Ministries, shows his fellow Catholics how to share their faith and encourage others by becoming mentors in faith"-- Provided by publisher.
Identifiers: LCCN 2021060574 (print) | LCCN 2021060575 (ebook) | ISBN 9781646801435 (paperback) | ISBN 9781646801442 (ebook)
Subjects: LCSH: Discipling (Christianity) | BISAC: RELIGION / Christianity / Catholic | RELIGION / Christian Ministry / Discipleship
Classification: LCC BV4520 .F755 2022 (print) | LCC BV4520 (ebook) | DDC 248/.5--dc23/eng/20220127
LC record available at https://lccn.loc.gov/2021060574
LC ebook record available at https://lccn.loc.gov/2021060575

I dedicate this book to three people who
took the time to disciple me and, in doing so,
raised me up to do the same for others:
Msgr. Brian Brownsey
Robert Kloska
Fr. John Ignatius, SCJ

Contents

Introduction

The Theory of One

In *The Art of Forming Young Disciples: Why Youth Ministries Aren't Working and What to Do about It,* I wrote about why the models of youth formation currently used in most Catholic institutions are not only inefficient but largely ineffective in meeting the basic spiritual needs of young people. Because their needs are not being met within their parish communities, young people are leaving the Catholic Church in droves. In *The Art of Forming Young Disciples,* I share the tremendous success I have had by shifting my parish youth ministry approach from a large youth group model into a ministry focused on small-group discipleship.

It makes sense that a discipleship model for ministry—where a couple of mentors work with a handful of people over a lengthy period—would be more successful than a large-group model. Our relationships within contemporary culture have radically changed. In the past, if we wanted to be part of a large-group community, we had to go to a location where a large number of people gathered (i.e., church). Smartphones and social media changed this reality. Now, nearly everyone in the Western world is connected with a large community, or often several, at all times. Finding large-group community is no longer the felt need it once was. The hunger in today's culture is for more intimate relationships—the kind of relationships that cannot be formed through a digital device. These relationships are best fostered in a comfortable environment with a handful of people.

Since *The Art of Forming Young Disciples* was published in 2018, I have given seminars on small-group ministry all over the country. The most frequent question that I get is, "If we are leading, what do we do with the people in our small group?" When I receive this question, I know that the person who is asking me the question is looking for a program. I understand this desire. Following a video study, a scripted leader guide, or a formation process is safe. A program doesn't often require us to invest in the lives of other people, and we never have to trouble ourselves with discovering another person's wounds, pain, crosses, and sin. Programs can be excellent tools to facilitate healthy discussion in a small group, but a program cannot provide discipleship. A program doesn't provide relationships and mentorship. Jesus invites his disciples to "put out into deep water" (Lk 5:4). For relationships to go deeper, a person has to be in tune with the needs of another individual.

The Theory of One

When I give seminars for ministry leaders, I frequently take them through an exercise designed to help them reevaluate their methods and approach to ministry. In the exercise, I present the following scenario:

> Imagine your pastor comes to you tomorrow and tells you that he wants you to accept a new position that he is hiring for in the parish. This job is so important that he is going to double your salary. If you are currently working for the parish, your current job description is now going to be someone else's responsibility. If you are a volunteer, your other apostolates are now the responsibility of someone else. The message that your pastor is giving you is clear: This new parish position is of great value to the community and he wants your undivided attention to be focused on this one job. Your new job is to make *one* lifelong follower of Jesus Christ and his Church.

The theory behind this proposal is that forming disciples—dynamic, Spirit-filled, lifelong followers of Jesus Christ and his Church—is our end goal in ministry. The Great Commission of Jesus Christ was to make "disciples of all nations" (Mt 28:19). The primary mission of the Church is to make disciples. Disciples of Jesus Christ change the world for the better. For example, St. (Mother) Teresa of Calcutta or St. John Paul II had a greater impact on the world and the Church than one thousand mediocre Catholics. This is what I call "the theory of one." If we want to produce the greatest fruit and have the highest impact in the world, we need to first focus on the work that it takes to develop holiness within one individual instead of working on trying to minister to all of the needs of the masses.

Of course, the scenario where a pastor gives you this job description would never happen. It's simply an exercise that I use to get ministry leaders to think differently about the way they approach their ministry. The goal is to identify the steps that it takes to walk with a person through the different thresholds of conversion in their life.

How would your ministry look different if this were your only responsibility? In all likelihood, *everything* would be different from the way you are currently doing ministry. If a ministry were only focused on forming one person, the method of the ministry changes drastically. The invitation, the format of meetings, the environment where you meet, how you provide catechesis, the way that you teach prayer, and the intimacy of your relationship are all examples of things that may be different from a typically structured parish ministry.

Sermon on the Mount Mentality

The Sermon on the Mount is considered by many to be the greatest sermon that Jesus ever gave. However, nowhere in the scriptures does it say that the people who heard that sermon went on to become his most faithful disciples. The content of the Sermon on the Mount was important—so important that it made it into Matthew's gospel—but as far as we know, it didn't form its listeners into lifelong disciples. In fact, the only reason we know what Jesus said in the Sermon on the Mount is that Matthew wrote it down, and Matthew was one of "the Twelve."

Jesus had twelve apostles. Those twelve apostles lived with him and were mentored by him for three years. Those twelve carried the Gospel all over the world. Those twelve were his biggest success story.

Even among the Twelve, Jesus had three who were most important to him (Peter, James, and John); among the three, we could argue that Jesus was most focused on one—Simon Peter.

When I say that the Church operates with a "Sermon on the Mount mentality," I mean that the majority of ministry that I see is directed exclusively at delivering a message to the crowds. We look at the sheer number of people we are responsible to share the Gospel with and we believe that the most efficient way to make disciples is to deliver the Gospel message to large crowds. The message is prioritized over the method.

This is not how Jesus operated. God's big plan to evangelize the entire world was small in scope. After Jesus's Resurrection, Christianity and the Gospel message spread like wildfire. Within a relatively short time, Christianity had conquered Western civilization. Have you ever considered it curious that Jesus—who always had the intention of the Gospel reaching all nations—never left Israel? Jesus didn't look at the world and ask himself, "How am I going to deliver my message to every person in the world?" Instead, Jesus looked at Simon the fisherman and asked, "How am I going to make Simon into Peter?" Jesus focused on one person first and then he multiplied to three, then twelve, then seventy-two, and so on.

This is the principal message and intention of this book. Disciple-making ministry isn't started with big programs and large conferences. Disciple-making focuses on the needs of the individual and walking with an individual on their journey as a saint on this side of heaven. If we don't know how to form *one* saint into a dynamic disciple, we can never hope to make "disciples of all the nations," as Jesus commanded us. By looking at the formation that Jesus provides for Peter, I hope to demonstrate how an individual can go about the work of making disciples in effective and efficient ways.

Who This Book Is for and How I Hope It Will Be Used

When I first started to write this book, I thought I was writing it for ministry professionals. This book is indeed very applicable to parish ministry. If you are blessed by this book's message, I encourage you to give a copy to your pastor, other clergy in your parish, vowed religious men and women, youth ministers, catechetical leaders, campus ministers, theology and religion teachers, or anyone else in your Church ministry radius. That being said, the more that I fleshed out the content of this book, the more I realized that every Catholic could, and I hope will, take the message to heart.

My professional ministry background is youth ministry and small-group discipleship. In my parish coaching program, I help ministry leaders identify potential small-group leaders within the pews of the parish. Usually we are looking for adults who have been discipled (mentored by an individual) because these people easily grasp the concept of discipleship. The more I work with parishes to find adults who are capable of ministering to youth, the more I have come to realize that we have entire generations of adults in the Church who have never been discipled. I have also come to realize that there are many in the pews on Sunday who are gifted by the Holy Spirit yet have never been empowered to use those gifts to minister to even one other person.

My greatest wish is that you will feel empowered and encouraged to intentionally reach out to your neighbor and accompany that person on a journey of faith. Whether it is a formal parish ministry, a small study group of Catholics who use this book to inform their apostolates, or a single Catholic who reaches out to a neighbor, I pray that all of us feel the weight and responsibility of Christ's call to us through the grace of Baptism to "go, therefore, and make disciples of all nations" (Mt 28:19).

1.

Connect

The Disciple-Making Temperament

> If conversion to Christianity makes no improvement in a man's outward actions—if he continues to be just as snobbish or spiteful or envious or ambitious as he was before—then I think we must suspect that his "conversion" was largely imaginary.
>
> —*C. S. Lewis*

I saw a movie several years ago in which a story was told about a young aspiring magician. When the magician was a teenager, he approached the mayor of the town and asked him to pull a card from a deck and sign his name to the card. To the mayor's amusement, the boy performed a simple sleight-of-hand trick with the signed card. The mayor chuckled and congratulated the boy on his craft, and he went on his merry way.

However, the young aspiring magician had a much bigger plan than mastering simple card tricks. He took the card that the mayor had signed and stuck it into a hole in a tree. Over many years, the tree grew around the card, enclosing the card in the center of the large tree.

Thirty years later, the mayor, now the governor of the state, returned to the town. The magician was now a grown man and rather well known within the region, but the governor had long forgotten his interaction with the magician several decades before. The magician approached the governor and asked him to pull a card from a deck and sign his name to the card. Using sleight of hand, he made sure that the governor pulled the same card that he had pulled thirty years prior, and he made sure that the governor signed the card in the same place as before. The magician pocketed the card and then asked someone to cut down the tree in the center of the town. The governor was astonished to find that his card was growing in the center of the tree (of course, he didn't realize this was the card from thirty years prior). The magician instantly became a legend, and the townspeople spoke of his incredible trick for years to come.

What I find inspiring about this story is that the magician had an idea for an amazing trick that required him to be patient for *thirty years* to see it through to fruition. I wish that Christians had this same kind of patience and vision when it came to forming disciples. I often find that Christians who have a zeal and desire to spread the Gospel can do more damage than good when they lack the appropriate temperament.

If you were only responsible for making one disciple of Jesus Christ, you have the freedom to think long term and see the bigger picture. Every person on earth is given a lifetime to become a saint, and everyone's journey is different. We can see examples of the diversity of faith journeys when looking at the lives of different canonized saints. For some, such as St. Thérèse of Lisieux, holiness is a part of the narrative of their entire lives. For others, such as St. Dismas—who was crucified next to Jesus and repented of his sin moments before his death—sanctity happens at the very end of life. The key is that a person who seeks to walk with another has to recognize that they are along for the journey.

If you wish to make a lifelong disciple of Jesus Christ, you have to be committed to the whole journey. You have to be *willing* to accompany someone throughout their lifetime. This is a big commitment.

Accompaniment

If you work in ministry or you are at your local church a lot, you are probably familiar with many of the buzzwords of the present day. Terms such as *New Evangelization, discipleship*, and *accompaniment* are some of the terms that I frequently hear used in conversations with ministry professionals. Understanding terms and definitions is important because it helps us distinguish the kind of ministry that we are talking about in certain situations.

I once got a bit cross with a colleague of mine, Mark, when he misused one of these terms. The conversation went something like this:

> Mark: I recently read your book on youth ministry. You wrote a wonderful book on accompaniment.

> Me: Thank you. But I haven't written a book on accompaniment. I wrote a book on discipleship.
>
> Mark: Well . . . they are the same thing.
>
> Me: No! They are not! Discipleship refers to a method of ministry where a rabbi has an intentional mentoring relationship with a small number of selected people. Accompaniment is simply walking or journeying with a person through their life. Accompaniment is a necessary part of discipleship, but it is not the same thing.

I probably startled Mark a bit with my response, but I wanted to make a point. This distinction between the words *accompaniment* and *discipleship* is important. If we don't understand the difference between discipleship and accompaniment, we don't understand the goal of what we are doing and why we are doing it. If you wish to disciple someone, you accompany them so that you may understand them and help them to know that they are understood. A person will never trust or follow the advice of a teacher if they do not first know that they are understood. Accompaniment is the first step for establishing discipleship, but it doesn't complete the work of discipleship. (I will share more on the following steps later in the book.)

God embodies accompaniment in the Incarnation of Jesus Christ. God does not seek to save humanity by keeping a safe distance from sin and the flesh. Rather, God becomes flesh and enters into every part of the human experience (except sin). We know that God understands every facet of what it means to be human because he *is* human.

The one thing that Jesus did not share in was sin, and yet his temperament toward the sinner is not one of judgment. I bring up sin because Jesus's temperament toward sin is a necessary temperament to have if accompaniment is to be successful.

Jesus, Sin, and the Lepers

When Jesus walked the earth, one of the greatest diseases of the time was leprosy. If a person contracted this disease, they were forced to live apart from the rest of humanity because they were contagious. Lepers lived in colonies with one another and were considered "unclean." In the book of Leviticus, God tells Moses what is supposed to happen to a person who is unclean: they are quarantined from society because they are contagious; anyone who would touch them immediately became unclean as well (Lv 13:1–2, 44–46).

Jesus turns this mindset on its head. In the Gospel of Mark, when Jesus meets a leper, he reaches out, touches him, and says, "Be made clean" (Mk 1:40–45). Jesus does not catch the man's leprosy. Rather, the man catches Jesus's purity. Rather than Jesus becoming ill, the opposite occurs—the leper becomes well.

This is also an illustration of the relationship that Jesus has with sin and the sinner. Jesus enters into humanity but he does not "catch" humanity's sinfulness. Also, he does not keep a safe distance from the sinner and shout "Unclean" at them. Rather, Jesus is not afraid to touch the sinner because he cleanses each person of their sins. Jesus accompanies humanity by entering into our very experiences. He comes close to us and he cleanses us.

Jesus Meets Simon, the Sinner

Jesus's temperament with sinners is very important to understand, particularly when we consider his relationship with Peter. The first time Jesus meets Simon the fisherman (who would one day be named Peter), Simon warns Jesus to keep a safe distance away from him.

In the Gospel of Luke, Jesus performs a fishing miracle in the presence of Simon, who responds, "Depart from me, Lord, for I am a sinful man" (Lk 5:8). It is as if Simon Peter were a leper and he is warning Jesus that he is "unclean." Jesus doesn't keep his distance. On the contrary, Jesus comes closer to Simon and says, "Do not be afraid; from now on you will be catching men" (Lk 5:10). There is no judgment from Jesus and no fear of the sinner. Jesus doesn't keep a safe distance; he dives right in.

Perhaps you have heard the common Christian cliché "Hate the sin but love the sinner." The problem with this statement is that those that I have heard use it are usually light on the love of the sinner and they double down on the hate of the sin. This phrase is frequently the catchphrase of Christians who love to cast judgment on others because of their sins. It's like the person is saying, "I love you, but here is my loophole to justify judging you." This cliché doesn't accurately describe the temperament of Jesus. He did much more than what many of us think of as *love*. Rather, he demonstrated that love doesn't have a loophole. Jesus got close to the sinner. He touched the sinner. If we wish to imitate

Christ's example, we have to be willing to touch the sinner as well.

Our Pharisee Problem

If you read the gospels, there is only one kind of person that Jesus is ever hard on: the self-righteous scribes and Pharisees. These were the religious leaders of the time. In the Bible, the Pharisees are quick to judge and condemn and slow to help others. They think that they know better than Jesus, and ultimately they are the ones who hand over Jesus to be crucified. In Matthew's gospel, Jesus condemns the scribes and Pharisees, saying, "You lock the kingdom of heaven before human beings. You do not enter yourselves, nor do you allow entrance to those trying to enter"(Mt 23:13). Think about this: Jesus was merciful with the prostitutes, the tax collectors, the woman caught in adultery, the promiscuous Samaritan at the well, the pagan centurion, and the Roman soldiers who tortured and killed him. Who were the people that Jesus condemned? The self-righteous.

I am concerned by what I see in today's Church. I see many supposedly devout Christians who more closely resemble the Pharisees than they do Christ. I see bishops, clergy, religious, and laity who are more willing to condemn the sinner to hell than get close to the sinner. I see social media inundated with Catholics who sit behind the safety of their keyboards and lecture others about right and wrong while parish ministries struggle to find enough volunteers to run the simplest of ministries—ministries that actually help people. I see faithful Catholic families who try to create safe Catholic bubbles for their children rather than engage the community and witness to those around them.

I have been doing ministry with the faithful for a long time. In all my years of ministry, I have never met someone who has said that their heart was converted because someone lectured them on Facebook or Twitter. However, if you go on these social media channels, you will find all kinds of Christians condemning, insulting, arguing, and preaching down to others.

I have never seen a Catholic pro-choice politician who amended their ways and repented because a bishop or priest called them a heretic and punished them. Despite this strategy having a zero percent success rate, I know many Christians who want to see their bishops do just that.

I have never met a Protestant who converted to Catholicism because a Catholic came after them and harassed them with biblical rebuttals they learned from their study of apologetics. Starting a conversation with "Let me tell you why you are wrong . . ." isn't an act of love.

I have never met a Catholic community that converted others because they created a Catholic bubble where they could safely stay apart from all the world's influences. Jesus commanded us to go out and make disciples, not isolate ourselves from the rest of the world.

Anger doesn't evangelize.

Trolling isn't a ministry.

Know-it-alls engage no one.

Christianity is not a gated community.

What does work? Reaching out and touching the sinner. I think there's a reason that Christians are afraid to do this. When we reach out to the sinner, we communicate to them that "I am with you for the journey of your life, even if it means that I accompany you for your *whole* life." It's like the magician who waited thirty years to execute his greatest trick. Accompaniment requires a temperament of patience and commitment.

One of the reasons the Pharisee doesn't succeed is because he is lazy. The Pharisee wants to convert people without any personal cost or commitment. But the problem goes further than laziness. The Pharisee isn't invested in actually helping the sinner. He is happy to recite Church teaching and tell the sinner what they are doing is wrong, casting judgment and condemnation on the sinner. Christ doesn't do this. Christ carries the burdens of the sinner. Christ enters into the sinner's life. Christ shows mercy and seeks to understand and be understood.

Before we can even consider all the different steps that it takes to form a lifelong follower of Jesus Christ and his Church, we must first evaluate ourselves and our temperament. Having a temperament like the Messiah is the only attitude that works when it comes to forming saints in the ways of discipleship. Reaching our potential as saints involves becoming like Christ. If we are to show someone the path toward greater union with Christ, we have to first show them what it means to be Christlike. This means we have to be willing to reach out and touch the life of the sinner and accompany them on their long journey. This is what Jesus did. To be successful, we must do the same.

Do I Have the Right Temperament?

Take this brief self-assessment to help you evaluate whether your temperament is that of the Messiah or a Pharisee.

- Do I waste time on social media engaging in debates over religion, dogma, and/or faith?

- Have I insulted or cast judgment on someone (either in person or online) because of their sin, political views, or behavior?

- Do I engage in friendships or relationships outside of my Christian community?

- When I see someone act in a sinful manner, is my heart moved to compassion and pity for the person or am I immediately angered by their behavior?

- Does my heart break for the lost, the broken, the poor, and the sick or are these people an afterthought in my life?

- Do I allow myself to be taken up with the concerns of the world by mixing my faith with political views, conspiracy theories, "prophecies" about what is to come, and the gloom and doom of the news media, or do I keep my focus on Christ and what he is asking me to do each day?

- Am I engaged in a ministry that puts me in relationship with other people?

- Am I interested in being seen and admired for the good works that I do in my church or community or am I simply interested in following Christ?

If you don't have a perfect score on this self-assessment, meaning your behavior is more like a Pharisee than Christ, it simply means you are not "there" yet. Repent of your sin and ask for Jesus Christ to soften your heart and teach you how to be more like him. Make your prayer that of St. John the Baptist: "He must increase; I must decrease" (Jn 3:30).

Small-Group Discussion

1. Who do you know who has the "temperament of the Messiah," meaning that they are not afraid to "touch the leper"? What admirable qualities do they possess?
2. Describe an instance when you had a negative interaction with a Christian who acted in a manner that was arrogant, judgmental, or lacking in compassion.
3. Why do you think Simon begged Jesus to depart from him? Have you ever felt like the sins that you have committed were unforgivable? Have you ever felt unworthy of Christ's love?
4. Do you ever engage in judgment, slander, or gossip about others? How might certain relationships or media outlets "feed" this behavior? What could you cut out of your life to help you live more closely with the Messiah temperament?

2.

Call

A Personal Invitation

> Never worry about numbers.
> Help one person at a time and always start with the person nearest you.
>
> —*St. Teresa of Calcutta*

I've given a few parish missions during my years in ministry and I've hired others to come to my parish to direct missions. A parish mission is aimed at preaching to or instructing Catholics—primarily adults—in the faith. It usually consists of an evening presentation or a series of presentations given by a guest speaker or preacher in a local parish. They are often sparsely attended, which suggests that most people don't see the message of the parish mission as having much value for their lives.

In all my years of ministry, I have only once seen a parish mission that packed a church with people. My friend Chris Stefanick has a kerygmatic presentation of the faith that he gives in one evening at an event called "Reboot." I've never seen a better system to get people in the door than the strategy implemented by Chris and his ministry organization, Real Life Catholic.

Parish events with Catholic speakers almost always involve an overhead cost in the form of a speaker stipend. There are two reasons for this. The first reason should be obvious, as St. Paul reminds us in the scriptures that "a worker deserves his pay" (1 Tm 5:18). The second reason is that the hosting venue (in this case, the church) is more motivated to promote an event if they are financially invested in it. If there is no risk for the parish, there frequently is little motivation to go above and beyond to bring people to the mission.

Chris hosts a "Reboot" event in a different parish around the country each week, and the parish does not have to put *any* money down for the presentation. Yet his parish mission almost always fills the church to capacity. How does he do it if the parish has no overhead financial risk? Real Life Catholic provides the parish with tickets to be sold for the event (because a person who has spent money on a ticket is more likely to show up), and they implement a unique invitation strategy. Six months before Chris comes to give the mission, the parish must assemble a volunteer team of thirty to forty people to go out into their community and *personally invite* people to the mission. Each person reaches out to their friends, family, and social networks to invite them to attend. This approach results in a church filled to capacity, and very often more than 50 percent of those in attendance are not regular churchgoers.

When was the last time that someone in your church community sought you out and personally invited you to something at the church?

"Come Follow Me"

In the days of Jesus, *discipleship* was a word used to describe the relationship between a student and a rabbi. As a young Jew grew older, he graduated from school to school. When the student was old enough, the rabbi would either extend an invitation to the student to "Come follow me" or tell him to "Go and learn the trade of your father." If the student was selected by the rabbi, he moved into the rabbi's household to learn from his way of life. The opportunity to live with a rabbi was a tremendous opportunity for the disciple.

In Matthew's account of the calling of the first disciples, Jesus calls out to four fishermen (Simon Peter, Andrew, James, and John) and extends the invitation for them to "Come after me" (Mt 4:19). The gospel says that they left their nets and their father and *immediately* followed him. Have you ever wondered why they immediately dropped everything? It seems like an impulsive decision to leave their lives completely behind to become disciples of someone they don't even know.

When Jesus comes upon the four fishermen, they are doing the trade of their father. This suggests that their opportunity to study under a rabbi had come and gone. They were not the best or the brightest, and they were stuck with the profession of fisherman whether they wanted to fish or not. The words "Come follow me" represented a new opportunity for them, which is why they immediately dropped everything to become disciples of Jesus.

There is much that we can learn from Jesus's invitation. He intentionally sought out these men. He could have gone to the local school, like all the other rabbis, and simply evaluated the next class of students as his way of selecting his Twelve. Instead, Jesus goes to where the tradesmen are located. He sought out the first four disciples. He went after them. The underlying message of Jesus's unique invitation to the original apostles was loud and clear: "I want *you* because *you* are important to me."

The Power of a One-to-One Invite

In my first four years as a youth minister, I built up a large volunteer core team of adults at a small parish in Florida. I called every adult in the parish that I could think of and personally invited them to join our team. The work was exhausting because it took a lot of time to have one-to-one conversations with so many people. When I moved to Colorado to take over an underperforming youth ministry, one of the first things I did was address the lack of volunteers within the program. I had an advisory board to help ease my transition into the position (which, by the way, was a great help). One member of the board had an extensive background in parish youth ministry. I didn't want to go through the trouble of doing one-to-one asks again, so I sought his advice. I thought that there had to be a shortcut. He told me, "The only way to get the team that you want to help with your ministry is through personal invitation. You have to sell someone on the mission and invite them into that mission." He was right. It was hard work, but eventually I had a very capable adult core team because

I sought out and pursued the people that I wanted to have involved.

I have worked in parishes off and on for the past fifteen years. Whenever I have to submit a budget for my department, I always request a sizable coffee budget to ensure that I have money allotted for plenty of coffee dates. Everything I did in ministry—whether it was engaging youth, rallying parent support, recruiting volunteers, or having meetings with my core team—was done over coffee at the local coffee shop.

There is great power in doing one-to-one invites. Several years ago, I attended a workshop on fundraising for ministry initiatives. The fastest way to raise large sums of money is to go to those who have means and invite them to join in the mission of your ministry. At this workshop I learned that asking for money from a letter campaign yields a less than 10 percent return. If you call people on the phone to ask them to join your mission, 25 percent of those asked will offer a financial contribution. But if you do a one-to-one personal ask for financial support, 50 percent of those asked will give a donation.[1] People are more inclined to respond when they feel that they are important because they have been pursued.

How to Create a Culture of Invitation

Recently I was giving a parish workshop on discipleship during which we discussed the importance of invitation. The pastor of the hosting parish was new to his role. He told me that every Sunday, he saw a church full of people that he didn't know, and he wanted to get to know them. He asked me, "How do I reach out to all of these people to begin to develop relationships? The thought of inviting each one out for coffee is overwhelming." I responded, "You don't. Select one person at random each Sunday and ask them out for coffee. You may not be able to do this with every person in the parish, but your invitation will make a difference for that one person."

One person can't get on a personal level with every person in a parish. The advice that I gave to this pastor may not sound significant, but you have to start somewhere. The Church is supposed to be a community.

Imagine if every person in the pews of a church was attentive to new faces and the people around them. What would it look like if several parishioners at a parish took the initiative to pursue the unknowns in the pews or in the community? Invitation plants the seeds to develop relationships, and relationships are the foundation for evangelization and discipleship.

I have often wondered, "How many capable and gifted people are sitting in their fishing boats just waiting for someone to extend the invitation to drop their nets?" In conversations with other ministry professionals, I often hear them lament that there are not enough capable adults in their local communities to volunteer in their parish ministries. Whenever I hear this, I think to myself, "I am a capable adult. In fifteen years of living as an adult in a parish, I have never once been personally invited to do anything in my local parish or local diocese." Of course, that hasn't stopped me from serving in ministry, but I think the lack of invitation has likely been an obstacle for many others. How many people like me are simply waiting to be invited into the mission?

The typical invitation to participate in the church is too often quite impersonal and ineffective. We post advertisements in a bulletin that no one reads, or we advertise on the parish's Facebook page that has few followers. We justify this impersonal approach because we believe that by sending a general invite using a platform that could engage many, we are inviting everyone. This approach is about as useful as advertising a meeting by standing on the top floor of a large skyscraper and dropping thousands of flyers to the crowds of people below. Some flyers might end up in the hands of a few people, but for the most part, no one is going to feel invited.

Because it is personal, a one-to-one invitation becomes the seed to start and develop a relationship. Most people want to be in relationship with others. An invitation communicated through a bulletin announcement doesn't meet that desire most of the time, but a personal invitation does.

This is a prime example of how ministry looks different when you focus on one person and why I ask people to rethink their ministries with this mindset. If you were only responsible for one person, you'd be foolish to invite that person out for coffee using a bulletin announcement or social media advertisement. In all my years of ministry, I have never had a person turn me down when I invite them to join me for a cup of coffee.

A ministry that calls us to focus on only one person at a time begins with pursuit and a personal invitation. This is what Jesus did with Simon Peter, and this is the most effective way to start a ministry with a person. It doesn't matter if you are a pastor responsible for thousands or an everyday Catholic reading this book. If you pursue someone and invite them out for coffee, I guarantee you have done more to build up the kingdom of God than some well-intentioned large ministry's marketing efforts have ever accomplished.

Getting to Know a Person

Another key to the initial invitation is to have a genuine interest in the person's life. I recall hearing a story of a university president who wanted to know each and every one of the students who attended the small school he led. He had photographs of each student and as he would meet and converse with them, he would go back to his office, open their files, and make notes on the back of their photographs. He then set aside time each week to study the notes on the photographs so that he would remember details about each student's life. Students were amazed that he remembered everyone's name and what they were up to. He would often ask, "How was your history final?" or "How is your mother recovering from her hip surgery?" There was intentionality on his part to be invested in his students' personal lives. The president wanted the students to know that he cared about them.

The same kind of intentionality is necessary when you are getting to know a person in the process of discipleship. No one wants to feel like someone's personal project, and no one wants to be preached at. I frequently have had conversations with parents who lament that their adult children are no longer practicing the faith with which they were raised. They ask if I have any advice on how they can talk to their adult children about the importance of coming back to the faith. When we converse about it, I usually find out that they constantly talk about faith with their children and that tends to be a source of tension in their relationship. In their eagerness to bring their children home to the faith, they actually push them away by annoying and trying to preach at them.

My advice to these parents: "Don't talk about the faith. Go on a fishing trip, go shopping, or do some other activity that will simply build your relationship." Building a relationship creates understanding, and understanding is the foundation for deeper conversations to naturally develop.

I have a personal rule when I deal with my own extended family. I never bring up faith in conversation. Because I work for the Church and my extended family knows it, I am sensitive to the perception that I am the "religious one" and therefore I am unapproachable. Just recently I was at a family funeral where I saw many of my uncles, aunts, and cousins that I hadn't seen for a long time. At a family gathering after the funeral, I was conversing with some of my family members and one of my uncles used some bad language. He then turned to me and apologized. I thought to myself, "Does he think I've never heard (or said) a bad word before?" I don't bring up faith with my relatives because I want to have relationships with them and I want to be able to engage. I have had many in-depth conversations regarding faith with my extended family members, but I don't *start* these conversations. Because my family members realize that I am approachable and because I have invested in relationships with them, several of them have approached me with questions or seeking guidance.

If we are to be successful in helping another become a disciple of Jesus Christ, we need to foster this kind of relationship. We want those we mentor to feel important, comfortable, understood, and cared for. That kind of relationship starts with a personal invitation, and it grows through having an intentional interest in the life and well-being of the person.

The Importance of a Comfortable Environment

Meeting in a comfortable environment goes a long way to help develop friendships. Certain environments will generate programmed responses from participants. For example, sitting in a classroom environment will make a person feel like a student and they are likely to act accordingly. Meeting in a sacred space will generate a quiet and reflective response from a person.

If you want to engage in a friendship-building conversation, meeting in a comfortable environment is key. I frequently tell ministry professionals not to meet at the parish. Why? One of the least welcoming and least comfortable environments is the all-purpose parish hall.

Take time to consider and note the most comfortable environment available for you to meet. A coffee shop, a living room, a restaurant, or a local diner are all examples that you may wish to consider. When you extend a personal invitation, invite the person to join you in your designated comfortable environment.

____

____

____

____

____

Small-Group Discussion

1. How would you describe your personal connection to your church community, for example, "vibrant and full," "connected and purposeful," "on the margins," "lost in the crowd"?
2. Have you ever received a one-to-one invitation to participate in the mission of your parish community? If so, how did that invite make you feel? If not, how might a personal invitation make a difference in your engagement?
3. In what ways have you failed to invite others into the kingdom of God?
4. Who do you know who is inviting and makes people feel welcome? What qualities do they possess?

3.

Witness

Revealing a Lived Faith

> Modern man listens more willingly to witnesses than to teachers, and if he does listen to teachers, it is because they are witnesses.
>
> —*Pope Paul VI, Address to the Members of the Consilium de Laicis*

Not long ago, my son was preparing for Confirmation and First Holy Communion in our local parish. When we dropped off our children for formation class, we parents were expected to attend an adult formation session that occurred simultaneously with the children's class.

For the first class, the program's coordinator had arranged for the parents to listen to a presentation by a professor from a local Catholic graduate school. When I walked into the room, I was immediately aware that there were many parents who did not know one another. I thought this might be a good opportunity to build relationships with other parents within the parish. Unfortunately, that opportunity did not materialize.

We were told by the coordinator that the presentation's topic was Eucharistic Adoration. While the topic seemed a bit abstract given the nature of the program, I thought it would lead to an opportunity to pray in Eucharistic Adoration, and I was looking forward to having some private time set aside for parents to pray and adore. Unfortunately, this opportunity did not materialize.

Instead, what we received was a seventy-five-minute graduate-level presentation on the biblical foundations of Eucharistic Adoration. I was bored out of my mind. I have two degrees in Catholic theology, and I generally enjoy presentations with theological depth. There was nothing wrong with the instruction the professor, an outstanding professor of theology for graduate students, gave to the class. The problem was the context in which it was given. The presentation was tone-deaf to the unique needs of the audience. There was no discussion and no time set aside for prayer. As a parent, the last thing that I needed was to listen to a biblical exegesis on the Eucharist.

Poor Catechesis Is Not the Core of the Problem

As I mentioned in the introduction, my primary ministry background is in youth ministry. I have authored books and articles and given many seminars on why young people are leaving the Church. In my travels throughout the country, I have found the following attitude to be a common sentiment among many well-intentioned Catholics who believe they understand why youth have left the Church: *The problem with our young people today is that they don't understand the teachings of our faith. We need better catechesis. If our youth simply understood the faith and the depth of our teaching, they wouldn't be leaving the Church.*

This opinion is usually supported by anecdotal evidence where the person making the statement can point to an example in their own life or community of a person having grown deeper in their faith once they had a better understanding of the teachings. But what they frequently leave out of the equation is that those who grow in their faith due to quality instruction are almost always already in the "spiritual-seeking" threshold of faith.[2] For teaching to be effective, one must be open and engaged to begin with. Unfortunately, very few people fall into this category.

I find this sentiment is most common among members of Generation X (those born between 1965 and 1983). Because Generation X received poor catechesis, many of these adults believe that this is the primary problem with younger generations as well and that we simply need to provide "better" catechesis to keep young people faithful. It is true that Generation X received very poor catechesis. The Church went through a lot of confusion and growing pains after the Second Vatican Council and poor catechesis was common. But it is a mistake to believe that improvement in catechesis alone is the solution to the lack of faithfulness among our youth.

When I train ministry leaders, there is a reason why I take them through the exercise of imagining their ministry is only directed at one person. When we put ministry in this context, most of our current formation paradigms fall apart. For example, imagine that you invite a spiritually seeking friend out for coffee. During this coffee chat, you might intend to have a conversation around the teachings of the faith. But how would you go about having this conversation? If you turn your coffee discussion into a class for your friend, your intentions likely won't be received well.

Honestly, when it comes to formation in the faith, I can't think of a method that I enjoy less than traditional classroom instruction. When I was fifteen, my family had recently relocated to a new city. I had been preparing to receive the Sacrament of Confirmation because my home parish offered the sacrament when youth were in tenth grade. In my new hometown, I had missed the window because my new diocese offered the Sacrament of Confirmation in eighth grade and I was already in the ninth grade. The solution that our new parish offered was to throw me in with the catechumens in RCIA (Rite of Christian Initiation for Adults). This program is for adults who are preparing to be baptized and fully initiated into the Catholic Church. I did not belong in this program.

I recall attending my first RCIA class with my dad. I sat in a classroom for ninety minutes while a priest went over different dogmas of the Catholic Church. I was already very familiar with these dogmas because I had been raised in a Catholic school. There was no discussion or emphasis on relationship building.

When I walked out of the class, my dad asked me what I thought of it and I said, "It was really boring." My dad responded, "Yeah. It was nothing but dry dogma."

That was the problem. The teaching was dry. Or rather, the presentation was dead. Jesus promised that he came "that [we] might have life and have it more abundantly" (Jn 10:10). The Gospel is supposed to bring life. Simply talking about dogma strips the Gospel of its power.

The Faith Is Meant to Be Lived

There is no question that Jesus was a teacher. He spent time in the Temple and synagogues teaching and sharing parables. However, if we look at the way that Jesus formed Peter and the apostles, very little of the four gospels is spent on Jesus providing traditional instruction. In fact, one might say that Jesus intentionally held back in the instruction of the apostles so that he could respect the process and spiritual journeys that they were on.

Think about it: Jesus doesn't directly tell the apostles what will transpire in their lives. If Jesus had told Peter, "Come, follow me, and one day you will walk on water and perform miracles, and you will have a high place of honor when I come into my eternal kingdom," Simon the fisherman may not have followed. These promises would have sounded incredible to an everyday Jew, and Simon may have either been intimidated to follow Christ because he didn't feel worthy or he may have written off Jesus altogether. If Jesus had said to Simon the fisherman, "Come, follow me, and you will be hated by your own people, persecuted because of me, hunted by the Pharisees, and one day crucified upside down in Rome," Simon the fisherman almost certainly wouldn't have followed. Jesus doesn't reveal the whole truth of revelation up front with Simon Peter. Jesus frequently leaves the apostles puzzled and wondering. It isn't until after the Resurrection that the apostles receive the answers to many of the questions that they had been holding on to for years.

The primary way that Jesus forms Simon Peter into sainthood is through shared experiences and witness. The apostles witness Jesus performing miracles and driving out demons. Then Jesus gives the apostles power and asks them to do the same (Lk 9:1).

Another example of learning through experiences is how Jesus prepares the apostles to accept his difficult teachings on the Eucharist. Jesus doesn't merely communicate the bread-of-life teachings to the apostles. Just before Jesus's proclamation that his followers must eat his flesh and drink his blood (Jn 6:22–59), Jesus demonstrates that he has power over bread in the feeding of five thousand (Jn 6:1–15) and power over his body when he walks on water (Jn 6:16–21). The apostles had encounters with Jesus that the crowds (who left Jesus) didn't have.

Before the Transfiguration of Jesus on the mountain, Jesus doesn't give Peter, James, and John an explanation of what is going to happen (Lk 9:28–36). He simply invites them to join him on the mountain to pray. When Jesus changes in appearance and Moses and Elijah appear before the three apostles, they are confused as to what to do because they don't understand what is happening. They experience the Transfiguration together and the explanation and understanding come later.

Perhaps my favorite example of Jesus relying on shared experience to teach the apostles is when he appears to the apostles on the shore after the

Resurrection. Peter and several of the other disciples had fished in a boat all night and caught nothing. In the morning, Jesus appears to them on the shore and tells them to cast their nets once more over the right side of their boats. They immediately catch so many fish that they struggle to pull in the nets. Peter, realizing that it is Jesus on the shore, immediately jumps out of the boat and swims to shore to meet him (Jn 21:1–14).

It says in John's gospel that none of the disciples dared to ask him, "Who are you?" because they realized it was the Lord. You would think that the disciples would have recognized him based on his appearance, but they didn't because Jesus appeared in his resurrected body. He did not have the same appearance. How did they recognize him? Peter knew that it was Jesus because they had shared this exact same experience together when Jesus had called Simon Peter to come and follow him (Mt 4:19). Because they had lived with Christ and experienced much with him, they recognized him within their shared experiences.

Throughout the gospels, Jesus focuses on shared experience and witness over mere cognitive instruction. Jesus shares meals with the apostles, celebrates Jewish feast days with them, does ministry with them, performs miracles in front of them, and gives them glimpses into the divine plan. It isn't until after the Resurrection that Jesus pieces together all of his teachings for the apostles and helps them to make sense of their experiences.

Experience and Witness

I began to develop a relationship with Jesus Christ when I was sixteen. One person who had a great impact on my faith formation was a priest named Fr. Brian. I had recently attended a high school retreat and had become moderately involved in my Catholic community youth ministry. Fr. Brian was the chaplain for the program, and he had a reputation for being very personable and likable.

Fr. Brian approached me and a couple of my friends about joining him for a road trip. He told us that he wanted to share something with us. My friends and I piled into his SUV and traveled ninety minutes to a Catholic parish where Fr. Brian had previously ministered on a parish assignment. We joined the Thursday-night "Praise Hour," which was a youth group that he started that centered around praise and worship and Eucharistic Adoration. This youth ministry was one of the simplest and most effective ministries that I have ever seen. There were about thirty teens who joined together in a small Eucharistic chapel. Fr. Brian spent the first forty minutes hearing Confessions during the Holy Hour. In the last twenty minutes, he shared the Sunday gospel reading and gave a brief youth-focused homily. After Benediction, most of us went over to the house of a couple of parishioners, where Fr. Brian asked a couple of teens to give a brief witness talk about their walk with Christ. This was completely impromptu, and the teens had no problem sharing how their lives had been affected once they surrendered to the love of Christ. Finally, we left the house, grabbed some ice cream at the local ice cream shop, and piled back into Fr. Brian's car for the drive home.

The format was simple, and the formation method had a profound impact on me. Fr. Brian didn't spend time teaching me lessons. Rather, he helped me *experience* the Christian life through an introduction to the Eucharist, community, and personal witness. These trips to visit this youth group became somewhat frequent for my final two years of high school.

At the beginning of this chapter, I shared a story about receiving catechetical instruction on Eucharistic Adoration. This presentation did nothing but turn me away from wanting to participate in the parish and its programs. By comparison, Fr. Brian spent very little time doing formal instruction, yet he had a profound influence on me because he introduced me to an experience of adoration and a community that loved the Eucharist. I experienced Christian living and that experience changed my life.

I firmly believe that if you wish to make a committed disciple of Jesus Christ, you must lean into shared experiences and personal witness over formal catechetical instruction. The old cliché is true: the faith must be caught; it can't simply be taught.

The One Thing That Damages Faith More than Anything

If the faith is most easily learned through experience and witness, it stands to reason that the opposite would damage the faith of others more than anything else. The opposite of witness is hypocrisy. Jesus said about the

Pharisees that they "preach but they do not practice" (Mt 23:3). Jesus was extremely hard on the Pharisees because they were hypocrites.

Sharing our lives with others through witness and shared experiences has an impact in as much as our lives witness to something greater than ourselves. If Christians act the way that Christ taught, their very lives look different from the rest of the world. The preacher and author Francis Chan once said, "Something is wrong when our lives make sense to unbelievers."[3] People become curious when they meet a person who finds lasting joy and peace by taking a path that is contrary to the rest of the world. However, if they follow a person down that path and discover that the person they are following is in fact a fraud, the results can be devastating for that person.

This is one of the many reasons why the Catholic Church's sexual abuse scandal and cover-up have been so devastating in the Church. We will feel the ramifications of these sins in the Church for many generations. It is horrifying that terrible sexual sins could be committed by our religious leaders through their betrayal of trust and abuse of power. I might argue that it has been equally painful for faithful believers to discover that our episcopal leadership covered up these crimes for decades. In the case of the former, predators infiltrated a respected position in society and used the position to prey on vulnerable people. In the case of the latter, the leadership that covered up these crimes were incredible hypocrites, betraying the faithful and the vulnerable to protect assets and avoid controversy and embarrassment.

I bring up this painful example because a person who is walking with another needs to be sensitive to the wounds that hypocrisy may have caused in that person's life. These wounds don't have to be caused by something as major as the Church sexual abuse scandal. People come to the Church every day because they are in vulnerable positions, and it only takes one bad experience with someone representing the Church to cause deep-seated wounds that may take years to heal. I've seen these instances happen more times than I can count: a bad experience planning a funeral liturgy with the parish liturgist; a person who has hit financial hard times and they encounter a parish staff member who is insensitive to their situation. A deep wound can happen from a negative interaction with a so-called devout Catholic on social media.

If you are discipling someone and they share that they walked away from the Church because they were the victim of the sin of hypocrisy, you need to be patient with this person. No amount of catechesis or formation is going to bring this person back to the Church. They need to have someone who will listen to them, empathize with their pain, and slowly restore trust. This work takes time, but it is necessary if we are going to bring those who have been wounded by the Church back into the fold.

A Note on Catechesis

A poor explanation of Christ's teachings can also damage a person's faith. You will notice that I haven't devoted any of the pages of this book to discussing curriculum or catechesis. If your ministry is centered on one person, it becomes more difficult to follow a formation curriculum or program. This is a good thing. When you only minister to one person, the study of the faith (which is a necessary discipline for any disciple) becomes more of an ongoing discussion than a program. I firmly believe that after age thirteen, formal classroom instruction on the faith needs to be replaced with a format that allows for dialogue. Critical thinking fully develops by age thirteen, and teens begin to ask questions and challenge the lessons that they were taught as children. Engaging in critical thinking and answering the tough questions is part of the process of forming a disciple.

The Catholic Church in the United States recently commissioned a national dialogue with young people. This was a multiyear process of conversations with and about young people in the United States. Consider this quote from a survey of Catholic young people:

> Young people struggle with Church teachings. One last theme that came up frequently in conversations was how young people struggle with the Church's teachings (in 45.5% of conversations). While the teachings they take issue with vary, there seems to be a clear sense that they want to learn more and wish to engage in dialogue in these areas. Unlike some theories that better catechesis would alleviate this concern, we observed that many young people really do understand the Church's teaching well, but felt that there was more to be said. Whether they agree with the theological concepts is one thing. What

> came up in many conversations was the lack of action or consistency in the living out of these teachings.[4]

The report from this national study found that our young people weren't suffering from a lack of catechesis. They were actually hungry for dialogue, and they were troubled by the Church's lack of consistency in action and witness. I believe this could be said of all Catholics. Gone is the age where people simply trusted the priest and were obedient to the teachings. This kind of unhealthy temperament was common among baby boomers (those born between 1945 and 1965). It led to a culture of "clericalism," where a priest, put into a position of power in the life of the faithful, had no accountability. A culture of clericalism enabled the sexual abuse crisis. Our priests should never be in positions of power. An effective priest is in a position of service. Being of service puts a priest on the same level or even lower than the people that they serve. Being on the same level is necessary for dialogue. Today, people want to dialogue with clergy and understand the "why" behind the teaching. Establishing this kind of catechesis can only be accomplished through dialogue.

The final point I will make on catechesis is that we have a responsibility to be faithful to the original teachings of Jesus Christ. A battle between the fidelity to the truth of the gospel versus fidelity to the "spirit of the times" has been ongoing for decades as some in the Church are fighting for "reforms" that will update the Church to align with the "spirit of the times." I need to make a distinction here between dogma and discipline. The teachings of Christ never change. They were given to us by God, and we do not have the authority to change them. This is different from the disciplines of the Church. The Second Vatican Council, our recent ecumenical council, sought to update the Church's disciplines to align with modern times. We need to constantly reevaluate whether our disciplines as a Church are still relevant to the needs of the current age. The Church did not, however, change the teachings that were handed down by Christ. Communicating with the modern world is a good thing. Crafting and "updating" our teaching according to the prevalent thinking of the modern world is not.

One of the things that I appreciate about the universal nature of the Catholic Church is the diversity of thought that falls under the umbrella of Catholicism. We have Byzantine Catholic theology, Thomist theology, Augustinian theology, and everything in between. We also have many different spiritualities that are represented in our Church: Franciscan, Dominican, Ignatian, Charismatic, and more. But there is no room in the Church for a pseudo-postmodern theology that seeks to stray from Christ's teachings to become relevant to the modern age because Christ's teachings are eternally relevant. Jesus said that we will know a tree by its fruits (Mt 7:16). The push for "modern theology" in the Church has borne no good fruit. The religious orders that pushed for reform are dying due to a lack of vocations, the Catholic universities that embraced heterodoxy barely resemble any semblance of Catholicism within their student bodies, and the Catholic ecclesial authorities in countries that abandoned evangelization to consummate a relationship with the "spirit of the times" have empty churches. Christ and his message inspire followers. People who wish to follow the path of "the spirit of the times" don't need a church to help them along that path.

The movement within the Church to counter this postmodern effort is also concerning. Unfortunately they have gone to the other extreme, rejecting the teachings and reforms of ecumenical councils, condemning the episcopates of any bishops who do not accept their extreme views, and quarreling with other Catholics over trivial matters such as liturgical preference. As these "radical traditionalists" have strayed from Church teaching in search of shaping a Church to be in the image of themselves, they have become the very thing that they despise. They are like modern-day Pharisees, dissatisfied with the Messiah because he doesn't act and teach the way that they believe the Messiah should behave. When we spread the Gospel we are acting as ambassadors of Jesus Christ. We do not have the permission of the King to change his message to fit our own ideologies or self-serving missions. When we struggle with his teaching, our responsibility is to seek greater understanding. Changing the message to fit our own mindset does a disservice to the people we are ministering to.

Effective catechesis can be summarized in these simple steps:

1. Witness the Gospel with the way you live your life.
2. Share experiences and immerse the person you are discipling into the life of the Church.

3. Be sensitive to the person's wounds that may have been caused by hypocrisy in the Church.
4. Be faithful to the teachings of Jesus Christ as passed down from generation to generation and protected by the Catholic Church.
5. Seek greater understanding when you don't understand the teaching of Christ.

Commit to a Shared Experience

If you were only responsible for the formation of one person and you wanted to show them what it means to be a Catholic, there are plenty of experiences that you could share together to engage your friend in the life of the faith. In the space provided below, list as many experiences/activities that you can think of where you could show a person what it means to be Catholic. Think about many different categories of Christian living: liturgy/worship, prayer, service, fellowship/community, tithing, social justice, study. When you are considering how you will form the person you are working with, consider some of these activities as part of the formation process.

____

____

____

____

____

Small-Group Discussion

1. Describe an experience where you were bored at Church. What was it that made it boring?
2. Describe an experience where the faith was alive, inspiring, and exciting. What made this presentation of the faith different from the experience where you were bored?
3. Describe an experience where hypocrisy or poor witness within the Church hurt your experience of the faith.
4. Who do you know who has given witness to the faith in the way that they live their life? What admirable qualities do they possess?

4.

Encounter

Answering the Question "Who Do You Say That I Am?"

> Neither theological knowledge nor social action alone is enough to keep us in love with Christ unless both are proceeded by a personal encounter with Him.
>
> —*Archbishop Fulton J. Sheen*

My friend Marc has a rather powerful story of a time when he can first recall an encounter with Jesus Christ. Marc was born with cerebral palsy, a condition marked by impaired muscle coordination. Because of his disability, Marc wrestled with questions of self-worth and self-esteem for most of his life. He was raised Catholic, and when he was thirteen years old, he asked a priest in Confession why God had allowed this condition to happen to him. Unfortunately the priest gave him a theologically inaccurate and pastorally irresponsible response. He told Marc that the reason for his suffering was that God was punishing him for his sins and his family's sins. Because of this terrible response, Marc decided to reject Christianity, and he developed anger and resentment toward God.

Several years later, Marc was accepted to a state college on a scholarship. He found friendship and acceptance very quickly within the party crowd. But, of course, the sad results of drinking heavily to find acceptance are predictable. By the end of the school year, Marc had a serious alcohol problem and he was on the verge of failing out of school and losing his scholarship.

Earlier that school year, a couple of evangelical Christians, Manny and Eileen, had knocked on Marc's dorm room door. They talked with Marc for a while about faith and Christianity. Marc was polite but made it very clear that he had no interest in Christianity. But Manny didn't stop pursuing a friendship with Marc, and he prayed for Marc regularly. He never brought up faith with Marc again because he knew that Marc would not be receptive. Instead, Manny made it a point to help Marc when he was too drunk and needed a ride. Manny visited Marc at the place where he worked, and he acted as a shadow for him throughout the school year. When Marc's life came crashing down due to the poor choices he had made, Manny was there for the emotional breakdown. It was then that Manny invited Marc to come to church.

The first time that Marc went to church with Manny, the pastor preached on the story of Jesus healing the blind man in John 9. In the scriptures, the disciples of Jesus see a blind man and ask Jesus, "Rabbi, who sinned, this man or his parents, that he was born blind?"

Jesus answers, "Neither he nor his parents sinned; it is so that the works of God might be made visible through him" (Jn 9:2–3). This verse and the preaching that followed spoke directly to Marc's heart. By the end of the church service, a change had occurred in Marc. God had spoken into the wounds in his life and Marc began to know how God loved and valued him. In short, Marc had an encounter with Jesus Christ and that encounter changed his life.

Metanoia: A Change of Heart

You will notice in Marc's story that Manny followed all the steps that I have written about up to this point: He had a willingness to walk with Marc along his journey. He didn't force the faith on Marc but rather invested in Marc as a person. He personally invited Marc at the beginning of the school year and then again when Marc broke down and revealed that he was lost. Also, when Marc expressed an openness, Manny didn't use it as an opportunity to merely instruct him in the faith. Instead, Manny invited Marc to experience the community of God with him. His response to Marc was "Come and see."

Walking a person through different thresholds in the journey of discipleship is a process. The Church recognizes that we don't become disciples overnight. A relationship with Jesus Christ can happen in an instant, but learning to listen to, surrender to, and follow his will is a much longer process. This is why the Church initiates us into the sacraments over many years. A person doesn't typically receive all the sacraments at once.

There is a tipping point that a person comes to when they are exploring the faith. Actually, a person can and should come to these tipping points over and over again. The *Directory for Catechesis* refers to this phase as the "first proclamation."[5] In her popular book *Forming Intentional Disciples*, Sherry Weddell refers to this phase as "spiritual openness."[6] Whatever you wish to call this, it is a moment of conversion, where the person walking with Christ realizes who Christ is and they experience a change of heart.

The conversion is part of the process of a person's walk toward discipleship. The Church recognizes that discipleship is a process, and conversion is part of the process. We typically don't receive all seven sacraments at once. Instead, the typical Catholic receives Baptism early in life; then Reconciliation, Eucharist, and Confirmation after the age of reason; and the Sacraments of Vocation in adulthood. Anointing of the Sick is given in times of illness and at the end of life. Through the sacraments, God gives us particular graces for particular seasons and situations in our lives. Even adult catechumens who are baptized later on in life and receive all three Sacraments of Initiation at the same time, go through a process in preparation for these sacraments. The Church is set up to accompany people through different stages of their faith journey.

The *metanoia* (a Greek word meaning "change of heart") part of the journey requires an encounter with Jesus Christ. It is a moment when God reveals himself to someone. There are many parts of a person's journey that we can control. Metanoia is not one of them. We can present opportunities for someone to encounter Jesus Christ, but ultimately it is up to God to reveal himself to the disciple, and it is up to the disciple to be receptive to that encounter.

The Moment That Simon Becomes Peter

In Matthew's gospel, Jesus asks his disciples, "Who do people say that the Son of Man is?" The disciples give many responses (Elijah, John the Baptist, the Prophet). Then Jesus asks, "But who do you say that I am?" Simon responds, "You are the Messiah, the Son of the Living God" (Mt 16:13–17). Jesus recognizes immediately that this is a moment of grace for Simon—the truth had been *revealed* to him. From that moment, Simon is changed. Simon Peter's path is no longer that of a fisherman or even a disciple of Christ. He is now on the path to becoming the first pope and being the rock on which Christ establishes his Church. Everything about Simon Peter's life changes with this revelation. Jesus marks this moment by changing Simon's name to Peter.

There comes a point in any person's life when they must make their decision about who their God is. The key to these conversion moments is that God does the work internally within a person's heart. We can do the work to help someone open to God, and we can invite them to an encounter, but we cannot provide the revelation of God in their heart. This is God's work. The metanoia happens when God *reveals* himself to a person. In short, conversion happens through an *encounter* with the Divine Person.

Christianity is not merely a philosophy or a way of life. Christianity requires a personal relationship with Jesus Christ. Over my many years working in Christian ministry, I cannot believe how many Christians are lacking this very foundation of faith in their faith lives.

John's gospel states that "the Word became flesh and made his dwelling among us" (Jn 1:14). God became flesh because he wanted to be real and personable with us. He entered into humanity so that he would be accessible to us. Those who met Jesus quite literally encountered God. The same is true today. Our God is living and personable, and those who are his followers become so because they have *encountered* him.

Truth Speaks into the Darkness

What do metanoia moments look like within a ministry directed at one person? Sometimes it can be as simple as inviting a person to an event such as a conference, retreat, parish mission, or well-put-together program. Over the last several decades, the Catholic Church has done a sufficient job of creating many different "conversion" experiences that people can tap into.

When I was a parish youth minister, I spent one summer offering a summer course for teens on St. John Paul II's Theology of the Body. One participant I had was a fifteen-year-old girl named Maria, who had recently experienced a profound metanoia and felt a call to evangelize her peers. She decided that she was going to invite a different friend to the Theology of the Body program every week. One week she brought her friend Tony, and there was noticeable buzz around the youth group. I asked one of the other teens what all the commotion was about and they told me that Tony was an atheist. I didn't think this was a big deal; this wasn't the first time an atheist walked into a church. Then they told me that Tony was a militant atheist, the kind that is obnoxious and highly critical of people of faith. When I inquired further, the teen told me Tony was at our youth program because he had a crush on Maria, and she had invited him. I smiled and carried on with the program.

The next week, Tony returned. In fact, he came to every meeting that summer. At the end of the summer, he pulled me aside and asked me what he needed to do to become Catholic. At first, I thought this boy must have one heck of a crush if he is going to abandon his deeply rooted convictions to impress a girl. Once we got to conversing, I understood more fully what had happened in his life. Tony was suffering in his life. He felt as though something was missing, that life had no purpose. He decided at the beginning of the summer that he was going to commit suicide. One night, he drove his car to the local high school and climbed up to the top of the bleachers where he planned to throw himself over the top and fall to his death. Right before he jumped, his phone rang, and he answered it. The call was from Maria, and she invited him to come with her to church the next day. He agreed, got back into his car, left the high school, and went home. The next day was the first day that I had met Tony. Tony told me that everything I had been talking about all summer resonated with him and that Christ had revealed himself. Tony was convinced that God was real and that he needed to become a Catholic. He was baptized into the Church the following Easter.

Tony is now a devout Catholic with a wife and a beautiful family. He serves in his local parish as a youth minister (Maria also serves the Church as a high school theology teacher). At first glance, it may seem as though

Maria or I did some kind of heroic ministry to save this young man's life. We didn't. Maria offered a timely invitation. I offered a simple religious program. But those were the tools that God used to reveal himself and his love to Tony. When it comes to conversion, God does the work; we are simply the vessels.

While conversion events can be helpful, they aren't altogether necessary. In my years of ministry, I have been a part of many conversion moments that have happened simply because I was patient with the person that I was journeying with and God put me in the right place at the right time. In many cases, I have found that my role is to bring Christ into the wounds that people carry in their lives—to speak truth into the lies in people's hearts.

The Brokenhearted Girl and Her Ring

I was at a youth conference on a Saturday night following a powerful night of prayer with my youth group. I offered to the teens that I would stay in the hotel lobby to listen and talk if anyone needed time to process their evening in prayer.

One teenage girl, whom I had been mentoring for a while, stayed up talking with me well past midnight. Christ was reaching into her heart that night and asking her to give him her brokenness. For her, this meant letting go of an ex-boyfriend and the broken heart that he had left her with. While dealing with a young broken heart might not seem like a big deal, for this young woman it was a very difficult attachment to surrender to Christ.

She wore a ring on her finger—a ring that she loved—that her ex-boyfriend had given her. I asked her to give me the ring.

"What are you going to do with it?" she asked.

"I'm not going to take it or break it. I just want you to take it off," I replied.

"Can I have it back?" she asked.

"Yes. Trust me with it. I just want you to take it off," I explained.

The conversation continued like this for another ten minutes; she was like the J. R. R. Tolkien character Gollum, obsessing over his precious ring.

But why? The ring wasn't important in the grand scheme of her life. She wasn't going to marry the boy who gave it to her, and therefore, it was unlikely that she would wear it for the rest of her life. Yet she struggled to separate from it because the ring symbolized a *desire* to be loved. It didn't represent love, because her ex-boyfriend didn't love her (at least not in the way that she needed). As a result of her desire being unfulfilled, she clung to that ring with a false hope that her deep desire for love could be fulfilled by a boy.

The reason I wanted her to take off the ring is that I wanted to separate her from that wound. She also wore a crucifix as a symbol of her growing relationship with Jesus Christ. I had her take the ring and attach it to the crucifix. My message to her was "Give your hurt to Jesus. Give him your desire and hope for love."

This simple exercise became a turning point in that girl's life. It may seem silly, but she found freedom that night that she didn't previously have. As a result of separating from the idol of romantic love in her life, she learned to go to Christ with her desire for intimacy, and subsequently she found that God would fulfill her deep desire for love.

The Young Man Who Didn't Believe He Could Be Loved

I spent a couple of years mentoring Brian, a young man who had been adopted. He was very attracted to the community of the Church but there was some kind of personal obstacle that prevented him from maturing in his relationship with Christ.

At a Catholic summer camp, we held an evening of prayer and worship that led into prayer ministry. When I was praying with Brian, I had an impulse to share with him that he was loved by Jesus unconditionally. These are simple words and likely something that we have all heard many times. When I shared this with Brian, he broke down sobbing and said to me, "It doesn't make sense. . . ." We stepped aside and talked for a while and I discovered that Brian had always felt as though there was something unlovable about himself because he was given up for adoption. He couldn't understand how a parent wouldn't want their own child. Even though he had wonderful adopted parents, he couldn't get past the idea that there was something about him that was worth rejecting. When he heard the words "Jesus loves you unconditionally," it spoke to the deepest wound in his heart. God revealed himself by speaking truth into the lies that Brian had accepted about who he was.

God revealed himself and a conversion of heart occurred in both these situations. Both of these conversions came about because of a simple conversation that occurred because of an intentional relationship that I had formed with one person. When you walk with someone for a long time, you will be amazed at the simplest moments that God uses to reveal himself and change the lives of others.

What "Conversion" Experiences Are Available to You?

The Church has used retreats, pilgrimages, and other experiences for centuries as a way to introduce others to a deeper encounter with God. There are all kinds of Christian experiences available today that may assist you in helping another to encounter Christ. These conversion experiences can also deepen your own faith. In the space below, list some of the opportunities available locally, nationally, and virtually. Make a commitment to invite someone to join you for one of these conversion experiences. Examples might include parish missions, conferences (such as Steubenville), retreats, pilgrimages, camps, service opportunities, virtual conferences, and visits or holy hours in an adoration chapel.

____

____

____

____

____

Small-Group Discussion

1. Give witness to your own relationship with the living God. When and how did you first meet Jesus Christ?
2. Have you ever been impatient with someone else's journey and tried to force an encounter with Christ before the person was ready? What were the results in failing to respect the person's journey?
3. Have you ever attended an event where you had an encounter with Jesus Christ? Describe the experience.
4. Describe a time when Christ spoke truth into a lie that you believed in the depth of your heart.

5.

Pray

Learning to Call Him "Father"

> Prayer is not asking. Prayer is putting oneself in the hands of God, at His disposition, and listening to His voice in the depth of our hearts.
>
> —*St. Teresa of Calcutta*

Several years ago, I was giving a seminar on discipleship to a group of religious educators in North Carolina. Leading into a period of table discussion, I posed the question "How would your ministry be different if your entire job description was to form one disciple?" After allowing for some table discussion, I surveyed the room and asked for some examples of how the religious educators would change their ministries if they were entirely focused on one individual. One woman stood up and said, "This entire scenario would be terrifying for me." When I asked why, she responded, "I know how to run a program, support my catechists, and follow a curriculum. But if my responsibility was to 'form one saint,' that would mean that I would have to be a saint. That idea scares me."

Bingo! I couldn't have said it better myself. What is the key to forming saints? We have to be saints ourselves.

I have heard from people who met Mother Teresa of Calcutta that a few minutes in a room with her was a life-changing experience. I have met several people who had the privilege of meeting Pope John Paul II, and they told me that the way he looked at them with great love stirred in them a deep desire to be better people. The message that I have taken from these stories is that saints impact the lives of others in profound ways. A mere few minutes spent with a saint can change someone's life. Meanwhile, all kinds of people spend years of their lives with me and I have nowhere near the same impact as St. Teresa or St. John Paul II (I still have a long way to go). Through the grace of God, disciples make disciples. Saints form other saints. It's that simple.

The Great Commission of Jesus was to "go, therefore, and make disciples of all nations" (Mt 28:19). Every Christian has a responsibility to go out into the world and contribute to this mission. Why don't we have more people who do so? If you are not living as a disciple of Jesus Christ, it is nearly impossible to be fruitful.

Being a disciple does not mean that we are perfect or that we have all the answers. Being a disciple means that we are sinners in need of a savior and we are on our own journey as well. The difference between a disciple and someone who merely looks the part is that the disciple strives to follow Christ every day. Following

Christ requires a personal relationship, which cannot be fostered without regular communication.

What is foundational to a life spent as a disciple of Jesus Christ, to the life of every Christian? A disciple prays to Christ every day. In fact, a disciple has a mature prayer life—the disciple knows how to listen for and hear the voice of God.

Prayer Needs to Be Christocentric

When I walk into a Catholic church, the first thing that I look for is the tabernacle. After locating the tabernacle, I immediately look to see if the candle next to the tabernacle is lit, signifying that the Eucharist is present within the tabernacle. From the moment that I enter until the moment that I leave the church, I remain distinctly aware that I am in the Eucharistic presence of Christ.

Given the significance of the tabernacle, you can imagine how I feel when I walk into a Catholic church and the tabernacle isn't front and center or easily visible. If I have to play hide-and-seek with the Blessed Sacrament when I walk into a church, I get frustrated.

Once, when I attended a national training conference for Catholic ministry professionals, I was incredibly scandalized when I walked into the designated chapel. The conference was held in a hotel, which meant that all sessions were given in all-purpose spaces. When I looked at my conference brochure, I was pleased to see that one of these spaces had been converted into a "chapel" for the purposes of quiet prayer. When I walked in, I saw modern art, a massive prayer labyrinth covering half the room, a "prayer wall," fountains, and places to light candles in front of statues. The tabernacle was in the back corner of the room. It had no art, flowers, candles, crucifix, or anything of significance around it and nothing to bring attention to it. The way that the chapel was decorated spoke volumes about the conference organizers' priorities.

When I asked one of the conference organizers why the tabernacle was neglected in the prayer space, I was told that the chapel had many different "prayer experiences" in the prayer space to accommodate the many different spiritualities of the conference attendees. It saddened me that the organizers of this Catholic conference didn't understand that they had created a space where the Blessed Sacrament was not the center of attention. The tabernacle, holding the reserved Eucharistic Body of Christ, was being neglected in this chapel in favor of catering to a kind of spiritual pluralism.

I emphasize this story to make the point that prayer is defined as an encounter and communication with a person. For prayer to be Christian in nature, it must be Christocentric. It is not an experience that we do to center ourselves or to make ourselves feel better. It is not a mindfulness exercise. Prayer is engaging in a relationship with the living God.

The Habit of Prayer

It should go without saying that you need to have your own personal prayer life. I have been active in ministry for fifteen years, and I cannot tell you how many people I know who are working in Church ministry and who are struggling to maintain their personal discipline of prayer. At times I have been guilty of this myself.

When I am recruiting ministry volunteers or interviewing candidates for a ministry position, the first thing I ask is for them to tell me about their daily prayer practices. I want to know that the person sets aside time each day to pray and that their prayer reflects a mature relationship. I take comfort when someone tells me that they are in their local adoration chapel daily or that they regularly practice lectio divina.

Whether one is a member of the clergy, a lay ministry professional, or a volunteer running a ministry, it is easy to lose sight of the end goal. Ministering to the needs of people can be exhausting, and if we don't maintain the discipline of prayer, we can very quickly become consumed by our apostolates.

When I have neglected my daily discipline of prayer, I justified my lack of discipline because I was doing work that built up the kingdom of God. I made my apostolate a substitute for my relationship with Christ—a recipe for disaster. I learned very quickly that a ministry built without a strong foundation of prayer can rapidly fall apart.

Once I realized that I had built my house on sand, I recommitted to daily prayer. As I was rebuilding my habit of prayer, I noticed that I had a great difficulty praying in the space where I worked. This is very common for ministry professionals, even clergy. You would think that working in a space where there is daily Mass and a chapel would encourage me to pray more. On the contrary, I find that working at a parish creates something of a force field around the chapel. I don't like to pray where I work because my relationship with Jesus starts to feel like work. When prayer feels like a job, I am more likely to avoid it. I have learned that I need to find other places to pray before and after I work so that I maintain a vibrant prayer life.

I also found that changes in my routine contributed to the neglect of my daily spiritual disciplines. I had a very regimented prayer life when I was in college. My college class schedule made my days very predictable, and this helped my habit of prayer. I got married shortly after I graduated college and I immediately found that I couldn't maintain the same practices that I had when I was in college. My lifestyle had dramatically changed. The same was true each time my wife and I welcomed a new baby into our lives, when I had a job change, or when my kids became old enough to have weekly activities. All of these life changes affect routine, and a lack of routine affects prayer. The COVID-19 pandemic is another example of how people's routines can dramatically change overnight. I had to find a completely new prayer rhythm when the world shut down due to the pandemic that began in late 2019.

So what are some of the markers of a mature prayer life? For a person striving to be a disciple of Jesus Christ, I would expect a combination of regular sacramental prayer (Mass, adoration, Reconciliation), daily personal prayer (scripture reading, Liturgy of the Hours, devotionals, journaling, Rosary, reading the lives of the saints), and an intention to grow in conversation with God. Simply spending time in God's presence is a good thing, but it doesn't necessarily mean that a person is good at *listening* for the voice of God in their life. A spiritual director can help a person navigate their own meditation so that they are more receptive and attentive to the voice of God in their daily life.

Regardless of what your routine is, you will find that ministering to others requires you to stay rooted in a relationship with Jesus Christ.

Imitating the Prayer of the Rabbi

If you are tasked with forming one person into a disciple of Jesus Christ, you would be remiss if your formation process didn't include mentoring that person's prayer life. Prayer is a necessary part of the Christian life; it is impossible to be a disciple without a relationship with God. Looking at the way that Jesus formed Peter, we can see what Jesus emphasized in the process of forming a person's prayer life. Because the apostles lived with Jesus, they would have benefited from watching his routine and example. It should be no surprise, then, that the early church continued the practices of communal life, the teachings of the apostles, the breaking of the bread, and prayer in their daily lives following Pentecost (Acts 2:42). The apostles didn't come up with this regimen on their own. They were continuing the habits that Jesus had formed in them, and they transferred these habits to the early Church.

When it came to prayer, Jesus emphasized imitation. This is implied in the Lord's Prayer. Jesus frequently referred to God as "Father." Referring to God as his Father caused a major stir among the Pharisees (Jn 5:18). Because Jesus referred to God as his Father, the Pharisees sought to kill him because Jesus dared to put himself on the same level as God.

When Jesus instructed his followers in prayer, he told them to call God "Father." Up until this point, only Jesus had any right to refer to God in such an intimate and equal manner. Of course, we understand now that Baptism makes us adopted sons and daughters of God, and when we are baptized, we receive the promise of our eternal inheritance as one of his children. But at the time of Jesus, referring to God as Father would have been a very foreign concept.

Jesus wants his followers to come close to him and to come close to the Father in intimacy. The term *father* infers that kind of closeness. But more specifically, Jesus teaches his disciples to pray by imitating him, even right down to the verbiage he uses to refer to God.

What Does Imitation Look Like?

For many years, I ran a youth ministry that was focused entirely on small-group discipleship. Rather than emphasizing one large youth group, I managed twelve small groups of five to eight teenagers that met with an adult leader once a week for discipleship. The groups stayed together for years, receiving mentoring from their adult leaders, studying and praying together, doing service together, and growing Christian friendship with one another. In addition to running my own small group, I mentored the adult small-group leaders. One of the things that I routinely emphasized was the need to "instruct, practice, and demonstrate prayer" within each small group. When my leaders would ask me what kind of prayer they should teach their teens, I would tell them, "Teach the teens to pray the way that you pray."

It was really cool to watch as the teens took on the spiritual exercises of their respective leaders. If a small-group leader journaled in their prayer life, I eventually saw all the teens in their small group walking around with journals. If a small-group leader loved lectio divina, I noticed that the teens in their group would crack open their Bibles anytime they had the opportunity to pray. The disciples imitate and learn from the example of the rabbi.

Why have I spent so much time emphasizing your personal prayer life, and what does this have to do with mentoring disciples? If you don't have a deep relationship with God that is rooted in mature prayer and routine, the disciples will have nothing to imitate.

When I give presentations, retreats, or parish missions, I frequently ask all participants to bring their Bibles. I always reference at least one scripture passage as a core message of each presentation that I give. When I do this, I have everyone go through the physical exercise of opening their Bible and finding the passage to read along with me. I want each person to actually have to practice opening and reading their Bible. I do this because I know that many Catholics can be intimidated by the Bible, and I want them to get past that intimidation and exercise the actual movement of opening the Word of God. This is intentional on my part—I'm trying to get the listeners to follow my example.

If your ministry were focused on the discipleship of one person, you would have to expose that person to your prayer routine, exercises, and other spiritual practices so that they could learn from your example. Open the scriptures with them, pray out loud together, take the person to Eucharistic Adoration with you, pray the Rosary or the Liturgy of the Hours, do praise and worship, and anything else that has helped you to come close to Jesus.

The Power of Intercessory Prayer

Because we are talking about ministry, I would be remiss if I didn't mention the power of intercessory prayer. When my wife was a teenager, her first job was working the cashier's counter at a Christian bookstore. I don't know why she applied to work at this bookstore because she was not a particularly devout Catholic and she had no intention of becoming one. At that time in her life, she had become entwined with a group of older friends that was a bad influence on her. One of the men that she worked with noticed that she was coming to work hungover. She frequently talked to this coworker about faith, though his conversations didn't influence a change in her life.

A year after she started working at this bookstore, my wife had an encounter with Christ and a significant conversion occurred. She told me that she found out that the coworker had been praying every day for her to encounter Christ and that is exactly what happened. I firmly believe that his prayer for her played a significant role in her becoming the devout Catholic she is to this day.

I know of several very successful lay ministries that operate with intercessory teams as a part of their ministries. They actively recruit volunteers to pray for their ministry and they send specific prayer intentions to the group to pray for. I believe the fruitfulness of their ministry is due, in part, to the work of the intercessory team. When I direct retreats or mission trips, I always make sure that our ministry and those serving are being prayed for by others. I even have several convents on my contact list for particularly challenging intentions.

I firmly believe if you are prioritizing growth in your own prayer life, demonstrating prayer to those you disciple, and covering yourself in the prayers of others, God will bless the efforts of your ministry.

Creating a Foundation of Prayer

In the space provided below, write down your prayer routine or the prayer habits that you would like to add to your routine. Be specific about the time of day, the method of prayer, and the location where you pray.

____

____

____

In the space provided below, write down the names of three people you could ask to pray for you or for specific prayer intentions. Make it a point to make these people part of your ministry intercessory team.

____

____

____

Small-Group Discussion Questions

1. What is your current prayer routine?
2. What practices have you found that have helped you grow in your relationship with Jesus Christ?
3. God speaks in many ways. Describe a time when you have heard God speak to you.
4. How might your prayer habit have been influenced by observing someone else's prayer routine? Who were they and what did you observe that influenced your prayer practice?

6.

Challenge

Finding the Courage to Step Out of the Boat

> The way to get started is to quit talking and begin doing.
>
> —*Walt Disney*

When my son Jude was seven years old, I started teaching him to play chess. He had always shown an interest in board games, and he was particularly attracted to games of strategy. Chess is a thinking person's game; you have to anticipate your opponent's game plan while also setting up your own. In theory, a seven-year-old novice shouldn't be able to outsmart a grown man who has been playing the game for a while.

When my dad taught me how to play, I recall that he periodically would make foolish moves that would tip the game in my favor. I realize now that he was letting me win. I asked him later on in life why he periodically let me win and he responded, "Winning is more fun for a child. I didn't want you to lose interest in the game. I wanted to keep it interesting for you." I think there was some wisdom to this parenting strategy. After all, I kept playing the game and I'm now teaching my son how to play.

When I first started teaching Jude how to play chess, I was faced with a similar decision: "Do I throw the game and keep it interesting or do I play to win?"

I decided to play to win. It's not that I am a cold-hearted father who desires to defeat and demoralize his children. I wanted him to use me to test his strength against my own. I wanted him to earn the victory and gain the satisfaction of knowing that he beat his dad when I was trying my best. I wanted him to see the challenge and conquer the challenge.

I take this strategy with all my children. Whether it's a board game, arm wrestling, video games, or any other competition, I want them to test their strength against my own. I don't let any of them win and my children know this. Perhaps this is a mistake on my part and I have set them up to have an emotional complex. If Jude ends up in therapy because I have scarred him for life, I'll edit this story out of this book in a later edition.

Jude now regularly beats my wife, his friends, and his grandmother in games of chess. He also has beaten me a couple of times. I think there is value in setting up a challenge to be conquered. At some point, the next step in a person's faith development is the call to mission.

Get Out of the Boat

One of the most famous scripture stories involving Jesus and Peter is the story of Jesus walking on water. Matthew 14:22–32 recounts how the apostles were in a boat crossing the Sea of Galilee and they spot Jesus walking on the water. At first, they are afraid because they think it's a ghost. When they realize it's Jesus, Peter calls out and asks to be invited to come out on the water. He doesn't know whether to trust that it is Jesus on the water, so Peter tests him. When Jesus extends the invitation, Peter steps out of the boat and begins to do the impossible. It isn't until Peter takes his eyes off of Jesus that he begins to sink. When Jesus catches Peter by the arm, he says, "O you of little faith, why did you doubt?" (Mt 14:31).

There are many interesting things to explore in this story, but for our purposes, I want to focus on Christ's invitation to get out of the boat. It is important to note that Jesus invites Peter to do something that only Jesus can do. There are many miracle stories throughout the scriptures—healings, raising people from the dead, driving out demons, and more. The only time that anyone walks on water in the scriptures is Peter in this story with Jesus. There is no precedent for a person who isn't divine to walk on water.

Peter is scared. When he asks if he can join Jesus on the water, Jesus responds, "Come." Jesus invites Peter to do something that has never been done before. In challenging him (and Peter challenging himself), Peter crosses a threshold. Peter does something that no one else has ever done before, and the story makes it into the canon of scripture. This moment gives testament to the power of God and what happens when a person follows Christ (or takes his eyes off of Christ). Jesus shows Peter the way to do the impossible. When Peter begins to sink, Jesus corrects him and shows him the way. Jesus tells Peter to stay focused on him.

Later, Peter is tasked with the mission of evangelizing the world, leading a movement that was under persecution and starting the Church that would change the world. That is a big responsibility, especially for someone who is only a career fisherman. We might even call Peter's mission "impossible." In the walking-on-water narrative, Jesus is teaching Peter how to do the impossible. He is telling Peter, "Step out of the boat and keep your eyes on me."

The Importance of Raising Up New Leaders

St. Paul tells us there is one Church, but it has many parts. He describes the Church as being a body with members of the faithful assuming various crucial roles. In 1 Corinthians, St. Paul makes it a point to discuss how the Holy Spirit has given everyone different gifts and that our gifts all serve different purposes for the building up of the Church (1 Cor 12:12–31). St. Paul says some receive a gift to be an apostle, some are to be prophets, teachers, or administrators. He goes on to name a litany of other gifts (mighty deeds, healing, speaking in tongues, etc.). When I give seminars to ministry leaders, I make it a point to teach on this passage, and I remind them that the Holy Spirit has given gifts to every member of the faithful. What they need to make Christianity thrive likely already exists within their community. Despite this, the vast majority of parishes and Catholic institutions are struggling due to a lack of capable leaders or a lack of resources.

How is this possible? How is it that the Holy Spirit has given us what we need to grow the Church and yet most of us feel like our Church is lacking what it needs? The simple answer is that our Church has done a terrible job of empowering and raising up the next generation of leaders. I see this all the time when I go to training conferences for ministry professionals. At most of these conferences, the speakers, musicians, conference organizers, and attendees are members of the baby boomer generation or Generation X. That's a polite way of saying that there is a lot of white hair in the room.

Look at your local parish. Who serves in leadership positions? In many cases, the people doing most of the work are those of an older generation. I have seen some parishes that have tried to fight this trend by having young people serve in liturgical roles (such as lectors) or even on the parish council. I would call these efforts tokenism. These are not meaningful roles for young people.

When I think about the Church, I am consistently bothered with questions:

Have we created opportunities for Christians to discern their God-given gifts and have we presented opportunities for them to put these gifts into practice?

Are we providing opportunities for our older generations to mentor our younger generations?

Are we presenting meaningful ways for every Christian to serve in the mission of the Church?

Are we challenging our people?

Just like my son and his chess game, or Jesus calling Peter out of the boat, I think people need to be challenged to grow.

We Grow When We Are Challenged

I have never met a person who raises up leaders better than my good friend Fr. John. I first met Fr. John when I was a student at Franciscan University of Steubenville, Ohio. At that time, he was the director of evangelization on campus, and one of his tasks was to assemble a retreat team of capable students and offer retreats for other students on campus. I had an opportunity to serve on a team with Fr. John, and I was amazed to watch him work. He constantly allowed the students to discern and exercise the gifts that God had given them.

When I served on the team for this retreat, we had an evening where prayer ministry was being offered for students. When a student would come forward and ask for prayer, rather than praying over the student himself, Fr. John would grab another student and ask that student to lead the prayer. Fr. John stood there, almost like a coach, and helped one student feel comfortable praying and interceding over another.

Early in my years as a youth minister, I asked Fr. John to lead my youth retreats. At the time, I wasn't confident in my own ability to direct an entire retreat by myself. He graciously accepted my invitation and helped me to plan the retreat. I learned a lot from him by simply observing. I also got to watch firsthand as he did for the teenagers what he had done for me and many others on our college retreats. His work raised up leaders within my youth group and their gifts became manifest in our church community. We did several of these retreats together, and as we would plan each retreat, I took over more and more responsibility. Eventually I was confident leading these retreats by myself.

When I look back at my formation as a youth and young adult, I can think of many instances where I had opportunities to serve the Church in meaningful ways. It is because of those opportunities that I am so active in ministry today. I learned what my gifts were, and I found through Christ that I could make a powerful and positive impact in other's lives as well.

Empowerment and Mission

One year, while working as a youth minister, my pastor asked me to plan a service project for the youth during the season of Advent. In the lead-up to Christmas, the pastor wanted to emphasize serving because so many people get distracted by the busyness of the season—the decorating and shopping, parties and gift giving. At the time, my youth ministry was focused on small-group discipleship, and we had twelve small groups of five to eight youth who met with their adult leaders every week for prayer, study, fellowship, and human formation. These discipleship groups, which had replaced our large youth group, were yielding all kinds of fruit. I didn't want to lose that small-group dynamic by putting together a large service project for all of the youth to participate in. I also saw an opportunity to feed a bigger growth objective than simply organizing the youth into a singular labor force.

For Advent that year, I asked all my adult leaders to work with their small groups to discern a demographic of people that they have empathy for. This discernment exercise served two purposes. I wanted the youth to become attentive to the needs of the people around them, and I wanted them to discern who they were passionate about serving. Once each small group found their target population, they had to figure out, on their own, a way that their group could collectively serve those people.

The results were remarkable. We didn't have one service project; we had twelve. Some teens decided they wanted to serve the unborn, and they prayed outside of an abortion clinic during Advent. Some decided to visit homebound neighbors. Some teens did homeless ministry by making and serving meals for a local shelter. One group of teen girls organized a parish-wide mother-daughter tea and they put on an entire Advent program. It was beautiful to see how the Holy Spirit had given each of these youth gifts to build up the Church, how the youth discerned who they were passionate about serving, and how they were going to minister to the people they had compassion for.

I firmly believe part of the process of formation in the ways of discipleship needs to be identifying a person's God-given gifts and working to provide that person with an opportunity to use those gifts to build up the Church. If we don't give disciples of Jesus Christ a mission, eventually their faith becomes more of a hobby than something that informs every aspect of their lives. Jesus gave the Church a very important mission—to go make disciples of all nations—and everyone is called to participate in that mission. Every Christian needs a meaningful way to contribute to that mission. If we are tired of Christians sitting on the sidelines, we have to call their numbers to get into the game.

In the introduction to this book, I presented the hypothetical situation of a ministry job description where your only responsibility is to make one disciple. I then immediately said that this job description is unrealistic. If we have a responsibility to evangelize the entire world, how could we take the time to focus on one person? How could we possibly reach all six billion people in the world when our attention is only on one person?

The answer: Disciples make disciples. Saints form other saints. If we send that one person out into the world and inspire and empower them to share in the mission to make disciples, they will multiply. That is how one becomes three, and three becomes twelve, and twelve becomes seventy-two, and so on. This is how the early Church rapidly grew. This is how a ministry of one grows.

Self-Assessment: Ministering to Others

Take some time for self-reflection. Answer these two questions honestly:

1. Who does your heart break for? (For example, youth, young moms, single parents, the homeless, the disabled, the unborn, the un-evangelized, etc.).

____

____

____

2. What ministry do you currently do (youth ministry, catechist, lector, sacristan, mentor, etc.) to help build up the Church? Be specific.

____

____

____

Does your current ministry line up with the people you are passionate about serving? Are you doing any ministry? Are your gifts and talents underutilized? When our hearts break for someone, it is a God-given gift of empathy. If we spend our time, talent, and treasure serving the Church and the world in an area where we have no passion, we are doing ourselves and the Church a disservice. Consider how you can serve the people you are passionate about and how you can bring the Gospel of Jesus Christ to those for whom your heart breaks.

Small-Group Discussion

1. How are you currently serving the mission of the Church? Are you actively working to make disciples and minister to people or do you feel like you are sitting on the sidelines?
2. If you were asked to identify a demographic of people that you have empathy for, who would you choose to serve and why?
3. Describe a time when you felt that you made a positive difference in someone else's life.

4. Are you attentive to the need to raise up new leaders from a younger generation? How have you worked to give others opportunities to share their gifts and talents with the world?

7.

Embrace Suffering and Hope

"Take Up Your Cross and Follow Me"

> The Christian ideal has not been tried and found wanting. It has been found difficult and left untried.
>
> —*G. K. Chesterton*

In Matthew's gospel, Jesus says, "Whoever wishes to come after me must deny himself, take up his cross, and follow me" (Mt 16:24). When it comes to discipleship, Jesus doesn't paint a rosy picture. His message is clear: "Follow me, and all roads will one day lead you to the Cross."

The most important lesson that I have learned in my life as a Christian is to embrace the Cross. When I was eighteen, I was dating a girl while simultaneously discerning the priesthood. I didn't know which vocation I was called to, and being that I had only recently given my life to Christ, discernment of God's will was a new concept for me. I was very much in love with my girlfriend, and both of us called each other to live lives of virtue and pursue holiness. Our relationship had been instrumental in my faith development, and I could see myself marrying her. Because I had a growing desire to pursue holiness, I became very attracted to a life of prayer and serving others in ministry. Naturally I began to consider whether I was called to the priesthood.

The Church teaches that everyone has a vocation. As the *Catechism of the Catholic Church* states, "Love is the fundamental and innate vocation of every human being" (*CCC* 2392). We all have a call to holiness. We also all have a purpose for our life. Discerning a vocation is different from discerning an apostolate. An apostolate is a ministry that you do to build up the Church. This is a calling, which isn't the same as a vocation. A vocation is who you were created to be. Discerning a vocation is the process of discovering how God will fulfill the greatest desires of your heart. Your vocation also lays out your long-term road map to sanctity.

At this time in my life, I was wrestling with the discernment of my vocation. One evening while praying before the Blessed Sacrament, I made the decision to take the leap. I decided that it was time to break up with my girlfriend and apply to the seminary. I offered my decision to the Lord and told him, "If this isn't your will, you have one hour to change my mind and you need to make it obvious."

I gave Jesus an hour because I was attending an RCIA class that evening. I was someone's sponsor for the Sacrament of Confirmation, and I was attending some of the classes with the candidate as a support. When I walked into the RCIA meeting, I didn't know what the topic was for the evening. As it turned out, the topic was the Sacrament of Matrimony. Our campus minister, Bob, was teaching and he spent the entire sixty minutes simply giving witness to how his marriage had been sanctifying for him. He shared how he lived poverty, chastity, and obedience within his marriage. He talked about St. Paul's call to husbands: "Husbands, love your wives, even as Christ loved the church" (Eph 5:25). He spoke about how loving as Christ loves has required him to consistently embrace the Cross and sacrifice for his wife and children. As Bob shared about his marriage, I realized what an amazing calling the vocation of marriage is. I realized that when marriage is done right, it strips a person of selfishness, requires a person to learn to forgive, and ultimately sanctifies the person.

God spoke to me through Bob's witness. By the end of that sixty-minute meeting, every part of my heart was longing to be married. In actuality, I knew at that moment that I was called to marry my girlfriend, and she is now my wife of fifteen years. It was as if Christ showed me both paths and said to me, "Matrimony and Holy Orders are both good choices. You could be happy going either way. But there is one path that you were meant for. Along the path of matrimony, there is a heavier cross that was made just for you. If you pick up that cross and follow me, I will show you what it means to love."

Hail the Cross, Our Only Hope

Bob played a significant role in my life over the next couple of years. In addition to being the vessel that the Holy Spirit used to show me my vocation, I was blessed to have Bob as a mentor in my life. Bob was an incredible witness for me in my faith. He was very well liked on campus as he was one of the most personable and nonjudgmental people I have ever met. A person's worldview or philosophy of life wasn't an obstacle for Bob; he was always up for a good conversation. He would sit down and dialogue with anyone.

Several months after that RCIA meeting, Bob was diagnosed with Hodgkin's lymphoma. At that time in his life, he had three young children and his wife was expecting their fourth. To make room for their growing family, he and his wife had bought a new home and were in the middle of a major remodel. In addition, Bob worked late hours on a college campus to accommodate the college students' late-night tendencies. All of this is to say that it was an especially inconvenient time to bear the cross of a major life-threatening illness. That is the nature of the Cross. If we could prepare for it, it wouldn't be a cross.

Bob's suffering was very visible. The cancer treatments took a toll on his body and it didn't take much observation to notice that he was in a lot of pain. Over the past two decades, Bob has battled two relapses of cancer, and the aggressive treatments, while prolonging his life, have left him chronically ill.

Despite the pain that he was under and the additional stress that comes with raising and supporting a family, I never heard Bob complain. He didn't take a break from his job in campus ministry. He never ceased to be present to the student body. He didn't stop smiling, cracking jokes, or laboring to build bridges in dialogue with students. At times it was obvious that he was forcing the smile. That made his outreach mean that much more because I knew that he was making a choice to be present and personable even in the midst of his suffering.

While Bob was battling cancer, I attended a retreat that the campus ministry was offering for students. Bob gave a talk about the importance of embracing the Cross, because it is "our only hope." During that presentation, Bob listed off all the physical, mental, and emotional struggles that he had been carrying over the past year. Prior to this presentation, the students hadn't known the extent of Bob's suffering because he never complained about his illness. The list was enough to make my jaw hit the floor. Despite all these physical issues, Bob went on to share how cancer had been an enormous blessing in his life and how, if given the choice, he wouldn't have chosen to bypass the experience.

Bob's witness in his suffering made a big impression on me. Throughout my life, I have had to carry many heavy crosses. Suffering has a way of finding us—it is unavoidable. Of course, Jesus promised that following him would lead us to the Cross. In our discussion of discipleship and ministering to the needs of a person, this is the final and most important lesson to understand. To be effective disciple-makers, we need to give witness to the Cross and Resurrection of Jesus Christ.

Going Where You Do Not Wish to Go

After the Resurrection, Jesus and Peter have a very intimate and personal conversation on the shore of the Sea of Galilee. During this conversation, Jesus asks Peter three times if he loves him. Jesus does this to reconcile Peter to himself after Peter had denied him three times. Following this reconciliation, Jesus refers to the final cross that Peter will be faced with. Jesus says, "When you grow old, you will stretch out your hands, and someone else will dress you and lead you where you do not want to go" (Jn 21:18–19). Jesus says this to signify how Peter would die. Approximately thirty years later, Peter was crucified upside down in what is now St. Peter's Square in Rome. He was crucified upside down because Peter did not wish to be martyred in the same way that Jesus had been.

Why does following Jesus inevitably lead to the Cross? The first thing to consider is that without the suffering and death by crucifixion of Jesus, there would be no Resurrection. When carrying a heavy cross in life, the most important thing to remember is that the suffering will not be forever. There is hope because the end promise is the Resurrection. We cannot live forever in eternity with Christ without first walking through the doorway of death. It is inevitable.

Then why is it that a good God allows us to suffer? Certainly he doesn't want us to suffer. God the Father didn't wish for his Son to suffer, and Jesus didn't wish to suffer either (we can see this in the agony of the garden). Jesus gives us a clue of the importance of the Cross in his conversation with Peter. Before alluding to Peter's final cross, Jesus asks Peter three times if he loves him. He then explains Peter's final cross. It is as if he is saying to Peter, "You will have your opportunity to prove it."

Love is a choice—the choice to will the good of another. It is easy to love when our circumstances and environment are comfortable. Our love is tested when things get difficult, and we are allowed to choose to will the good, even though it hurts.

I hate the suffering that comes with the Cross. It is always unexpected and painful. No matter what the suffering is, it's always easier to throw in the towel. It is easier to say things such as:

- I give up on my marriage.
- I'm walking out on my family.
- I will never forgive the person who hurt me.
- I'd rather die than continue to suffer from this illness.
- I'd rather comfort myself with my vice (drinking, drugs, pornography, etc.) than put in the difficult work to become free from addiction.
- This unwanted pregnancy will destroy my life. I'm getting an abortion.
- My life has no meaning. No one would notice if I were gone.

These statements, taken at face value, sound awful. But they are said by people every day. The attitudes behind these statements are rejections of the Cross. These situations reflect opportunities to choose to love and will the good of another. When we learn to embrace the Cross, these situations make of us true disciples. It is in choosing to keep going, to keep climbing to Calvary, that a person loses all selfishness and finds a strength and love that surpasses all understanding.

The Greatest of These Is Love

In the previous chapter, we discussed the importance of helping a person discern their God-given gifts and raising them up to serve the kingdom. St. Paul says that there is something that is even more important than gifts from the Holy Spirit. In 1 Corinthians, St. Paul says:

> If I speak in human and angelic tongues but do not have love, I am a resounding gong or a clashing cymbal. And if I have the gift of prophecy and comprehend all mysteries and all knowledge; if I have all faith so as to move mountains but do not have love, I am nothing. If I give away everything I own, and if I hand my body over so that I may boast but do not have love, I gain nothing (1 Cor 13:1–3).

A Christian without love is nothing. Love is learned through the Cross. This is why following Jesus eventually leads a person to suffering. The Cross teaches us and gives us the opportunity to love.

The sanctifying nature of the Cross and the promise of the Resurrection are the most important concepts to understand as a Christian. The relationship that is afforded in a ministry of one provides tremendous support when these crosses come. No one enjoys carrying the Cross. It is ten times more difficult to carry it alone. Even Jesus was blessed with Simon of Cyrene, who helped him carry his cross up to Calvary. When someone is carrying a heavy cross, a partner can provide encouragement, perspective, and even logistical support. This is one of the many reasons why Jesus sent the disciples out two by two.

Christianity is meant to be lived in community with others. It is in isolation that we suffer the most. When the Cross comes to a person you are discipling, this is when it is most important to reach out to them. We are tempted to isolate when dealing with suffering. We can sometimes have a misconception that no one could understand our pain or struggle. When we have a ministry focused on one person, we notice when they have gone missing. No one falls through the cracks if everyone has someone to help minister to their individual needs. When we reach out to someone who is suffering, we show them that they are loved and have value.

Carrying Your Own Cross

If it is important to be present to others in their suffering, it is equally important for you, as the person ministering, to be vulnerable and transparent in your own life. This can be very difficult. I recall having lunch with a friend who had served the Church in ministry for a long time. At that time, my life was a mess. I had all kinds of unwanted challenges that had entered my life and I felt like I was drowning. Internally I was wrestling with my relationship with God and struggling to make sense of my suffering. Despite this, I was still serving my parish as the youth minister. I put on a happy face and shared with people how blessed my life was as a disciple of Christ, but I felt like a fraud.

Having lunch with my friend one day, I said to her, "I'm so tired of having to act like I don't have problems." She shared with me about all the times where she would travel the country giving presentations on the faith and then go into the airport restroom and cry. It's a very real problem for those who serve in ministry. The Cross comes to us and for some reason we feel as though we cannot show people that we carry crosses too.

In Jesus's public ministry, he doesn't hide his suffering. My friend Bob didn't do this either. Rather, they allowed their suffering to give witness to their hope in the Resurrection. They allowed others to see their humanity. Also, by courageously carrying their crosses, they give witness to the daily choice to love.

It's important in ministry to have boundaries and personal outlets apart from the people we minister to. We do not want to create an emotionally dependent relationship with a person we are discipling. On the other hand, it is important that our lives give witness to the reality of the Cross and that we are free to be vulnerable with others. Too often we paint an ideological vision of what Christianity should be and we don't give testimony to the purifying effect of suffering in our own lives. It is important to let people see our own human struggles.

I have known all kinds of people who serve in ministry (clergy, religious, professional lay ministers) who do not have healthy outlets of support for their own struggles. I believe this is one of the reasons why alcohol addiction is so prevalent among ministry leaders. People who work in ministry help carry the burdens of others, and in many instances they do not have someone who helps them to carry their own.

In my life I have found that I must have a brotherhood with Christian men in addition to a spousal relationship with my wife. At times I have sought out professional counseling to help me work through challenges in my life. I have found a lot of support from having regular appointments with a spiritual director to help me discern God's will in my life. I also frequently go on personal retreats to refresh and rekindle my relationship with God. Having my own support system allows me to continue to minister to other people and stay spiritually, emotionally, and physically healthy.

Who Is Your Support System?

Before you count yourself among those who are privileged to share the Gospel with others, take a minute to reevaluate your own support system. Ask yourself, "Who can I count on to help me carry my cross when it comes?" If you can't name anyone, I would encourage you to pray and ask God to lead you to someone who can support you. Two by two, Jesus sent them out.

Make sure that you are not diving into the deep end of ministry without a life preserver.

In the space provided below, write down the names of people who support you in your faith and who you can turn to for support when you have a cross to carry.

____

____

____

Small-Group Discussion

Don't be afraid to be vulnerable and answer this one question:

What cross have you carried in your life and what did you learn from your suffering?

8.

Toward a One-Person Ministry

> Our greatest fear should not be of failure but at succeeding at things in life that don't really matter.
>
> —*Francis Chan*

My friend Mario is a convert to Catholicism. He was not raised in any religion, and as a young man, he eventually found his way to Eastern religion and Taoism. He started dating a young woman who was Catholic and sang in the choir for the young adult Mass on Sunday evenings at the Immaculate Conception Cathedral in Denver, Colorado. Archbishop Charles Chaput noticed that Mario had become a regular at Mass and they struck up a conversation after Mass. This conversation eventually led to the two of them having lunch together. When the archbishop found out that Mario wasn't a Christian, he invited Mario to join him for lunch every week. Their friendship grew, and they frequently conversed about religion, philosophy, and Jesus Christ. Through his friendship with the archbishop, Mario discovered that everything he loved about Taoism was fulfilled within the person of Jesus Christ. Archbishop Chaput baptized Mario into the Catholic Church and they remain close to this day.

I love Mario's conversion story because it shows that discipleship really is that simple. Archbishop Chaput noticed a young man, made himself open to and available for spiritual friendship, and walked with him into a relationship with Jesus Christ. I assume that the archbishop is a busy man, yet despite his busy schedule, he made the time to disciple one person. If the archbishop can find the time to make discipleship a priority, so can you and so can I.

How Would a Ministry of One Be Different?

Let's look at the steps to forming a ministry of one. A ministry directed at one person requires the temperament of the Messiah and the intention to accompany the sinner. It requires a personal invitation and a desire to build a foundation of friendship. If you are only focusing on one person, the formation approach would lean heavily on dialogue, discussion, personal witness, and shared faith experiences. An encounter with Christ is necessary and this personal revelation could be assisted by inviting the would-be-disciple to conversion/encounter experiences. A faith-based relationship also includes an invitation to grow a mature prayer life. Building the kingdom of God means preparing a person to be sent out to use their gifts to minister to others. Finally, forming a dynamic, committed disciple of Jesus Christ requires assisting them with the crosses that they bear in their life.

When I think of the everyday Catholic that I meet in a parish, I know very few people who have received this kind of support in their lives. This is why we struggle to make lifelong disciples of Jesus Christ. Most of us don't know how, because no one invested this kind of time and attention in each of us. When I train people in discipleship—particularly older generations—I find that the language of discipleship is foreign to them. They have never experienced this kind of ministry, so when they are called into active roles in their community, they default to what they know, which means that they fall back on the same failed ministry paradigms that have been failing us for decades (if not centuries).

The change starts with you. In this final chapter, I will discuss a few different ways that discipleship-focused ministry could be implemented within a parish or a faith community. It doesn't require a whole parish movement to work. It starts with a movement of one. If you, the reader of this book, take the message to heart, you will not wait for your bishop, pastor, director of religious education, Catholic school principal, youth minister, or any other ministry professional to call you into action. Your neighbor is right next door. We need laborers in the vineyard who will answer the call to go and make disciples of all nations. That process can start with the simple act of inviting your neighbor out to lunch.

What a Ministry of One Could Look Like

Who does your heart break for? This is a good question to ask to assist in identifying a person you might start to disciple. Jesus had compassion and empathy for the sinners and the sick with whom he came into contact. The temperament of the Messiah is born out of an attitude of empathy. If you are a Catholic who sits behind your computer screen and throws stones at sinners, turn off your screen and go spend time with some real people. Allow your heart to break and you will find a person you can actually help. Take a moment to consider who your heart breaks for. Here are some examples:

- Young moms and / or dads
- Single moms and / or dads
- Young people
- The poor
- People who are homebound or those in nursing homes
- The homeless
- The elderly
- Parents of special-needs kids
- Prostitutes

Yes, that last one on the list says *prostitutes*. I know a Catholic deacon whose heart broke for male prostitutes who were homeless and living on the streets of Chicago. He struck up a conversation with a male prostitute one evening when he offered to give him a ride to a local homeless shelter. The man told him that he didn't want to go to the homeless shelter because the other homeless would abuse and ostracize him because he was a prostitute. As the man shared his story, the Catholic deacon's heart broke. This eventually led him to found Emmaus, a ministry that does tremendous missionary work with male prostitutes in Chicago.

No one is asking you to start a new missionary ministry (except maybe God . . . but one step at a time). Start by considering who your heart breaks for and identify one person who falls into that category. Next, invite that person to join you in a comfortable setting. Some spots that come to mind are your living room, a coffee shop, a local bar or restaurant, or even a park. Pray for the person and for the Holy Spirit to move their heart.

If your relationship doesn't click right away, remember that this is a marathon. I work with young people. Believe me, I have to work hard for their trust and affection. Once you have their affection, the work becomes much easier. As the old saying goes, "If they love you, they will follow you anywhere." As the relationship progresses, faith-based discussions, intentional study, shared prayer, and activities intended to build fellowship will likely become a staple of the relationship.

If your diocese, parish, or community is offering a retreat, presentation, or mission, don't go alone! Take someone with you. Make it a night out. Take your friend out for dinner and drinks and then attend the encounter experience together. These kinds of opportunities can lead to all kinds of threshold-crossing moments in a person's life.

Finally, be attentive to the God-given gifts of the person you are mentoring. The kingdom of God greatly needs more laborers in the vineyard. Don't allow the person you are mentoring to sit on the sidelines. Our faith is not a spectator sport. We need to send disciples out into the world.

What a Parish Movement Could Look Like

Think back to the introduction of this book. The premise of this book was built on the exercise that I use to get ministry professionals to think differently about the ministries that they run. If you are a pastor, religious, or lay professional, take a moment to consider how you are currently doing ministry and compare those methods to the ones that I have explored in this book. In all likelihood, the ministry you are running now looks nothing like the steps that I have discussed.

The purpose of this exercise is to get you to think through the practical steps that it would take to walk one person through the different thresholds of conversion in their life. We cannot afford to call this process unrealistic, too time-consuming, or, for one reason or another, something we can't do. If this process, with these steps, is what it takes to make a lifelong follower of Jesus Christ, then logically any ministry that does anything less than what I have discussed will inevitably fail.

If you are a ministry professional (a director of religious education, youth minister, and the like), take some time to consider each of the seven steps that I have discussed in this book. Ask yourself, "Where is our ministry falling short? Which of these seven steps are we not executing?" It very well could be that your ministry misses on all seven. If that is the case, it is time to scrap the ministry and start over. John the Baptist was very clear regarding what is to be done to a tree that is bearing no fruit: burn it to the ground (Mt 3:10).

If you are a catechist, small-group leader, or volunteer in any kind of ministry, I encourage you to ask whether discipleship is happening in your current ministry. For me, the reason that I started writing this book is that I do so many training seminars for ministry volunteers, and I find most of them do not grasp the concept of discipleship.

When we have taken the necessary steps of discerning what it takes to make one lifelong follower of Jesus Christ, we can begin to consider how to multiply that process so that we are making more than one at a time.

Small-Group Discipleship

I love small-group ministry, in part because it is one of the best environments to create individualized discipleship relationships. That being said, a small group of people meeting for a faith-based program—a video-based Bible study from a Catholic publisher, a youth discipleship program, a men's or women's group using the latest Catholic resource—does not translate into discipleship. Many Catholic parishes run small groups. Unfortunately the vast majority of groups that I see are based around a catechetical program. Many popular ministry books promote the value of parish small groups for parish renewal, but many parish leaders follow a catechetical program rather than entering into discipleship and their small groups fail miserably.

Programs can be beneficial as long as they are used as tools to facilitate discussion and encounter with Jesus Christ. Sadly, many of the Catholic programs that I am familiar with are overprogrammed and act as a strict curriculum rather than a discussion starter. As a result, the small group does not become a community where believers share in one another's lives. Instead the small-group meeting simply becomes another religion class. The real ministry that happens in a small group is not the curriculum on the page but the discussion and sharing of life that happens apart from the scripted program.

Alpha is one of the more popular programs available today. It prioritizes the basic Gospel message and delivers its message through short videos. The format of an Alpha meeting is to have dinner and table discussion built into each meeting. This is one of the only Christian programs I am aware of that intentionally builds discussion and community into their gathering. I believe that is one of the reasons why it is well liked.

The danger in running too many programs is that the small group can become a hobby or an exclusive club for some people. I have a friend who was tasked with building discipleship at a large Catholic parish in Texas. He noticed that when he offered a Bible study, the same core group of people participated in each new study. He also noticed that this core group did not contribute to any meaningful ministry in the parish. For this small group of adults, Bible study had become a hobby. My friend implemented a policy that those participating in his Bible studies could not attend more than three without volunteering for the parish in a meaningful way. He told them, "I am not forming you in the faith so that you can go home and keep the Gospel to yourself. That mindset helps no one. I want you to build the kingdom of God."

Don't get me wrong: I do not want my constructive criticism of small-group programs to be misinterpreted. I am a huge advocate for small-group discipleship. My book *The Art of Forming Young Disciples* is written entirely on the premise that the Church needs to abandon many of our current methods of forming our young people in favor of a small-group paradigm that models the way that Jesus ministered to the apostles. However, I am critical of small groups focusing on a program instead of discipleship. The real fruit of ministry is in the relationship between two people. If our Church faithful understand that concept, we have a much better chance of building successful ministries that meet the pastoral needs of the people we serve.

There Is Hard Work Ahead, So Keep It Simple

How do we create a movement of discipleship? When I offer parish coaching, I aim to keep the bar low. I want the goals to feel achievable, and I do not want the work to feel like a burden. If the goals feel achievable, there are no excuses for failing to meet the goals. Evangelizing the entire world seems like an impossible goal. Meeting the pastoral needs of an entire parish and local community is also daunting. It does not matter if you are one person, one small parish staff, or a mega parish, the answer to "How do we create a movement of discipleship?" is always the same: start with one.

Every major Catholic movement or institution that I am familiar with has started small. The Church started with twelve men formed by Christ. I am always wary of a Catholic ministry that aims to have a big reach right away. I have never seen that approach work. The effort and resources always fizzle out. The work to make lifelong followers of Jesus Christ has to start somewhere. Start small and grow big. You will be amazed what God can do when you turn your attention and your ministry to one person. Thank you for your yes to discipleship and your willingness to walk with someone on their journey of faith.

Create Your Discipleship Road Map

Take inventory from the previous chapters and construct your road map for a ministry of one individual:

- Name of the person you wish to disciple:

- Where will you find them to extend a personal invite?

- Where will you meet?

- Resources available to assist with faith-based discussion:

- List of local encounter experiences available:

- Your personal prayer routine:

- List of intercessors:

- List of people who are your support system:

Compare and Contrast

If you are a ministry professional and you run a formation ministry, consider the ministry you provide now and how it differs from a ministry of one. Ask yourself these questions:

1. What are the encounter opportunities I provide?
2. Where does the ministry meet?
3. How does the ministry method allow for relationship, discussion, and dialogue to develop?
4. How is prayer incorporated into the formation process?
5. How does the ministry provide support for those who are hurting?
6. Does the ministry that I provide for the many look anything like the way that I would minister to a single person? If the answer is no, it may be time to reevaluate your ministry and change the structure with the individual needs of a person in mind.

Small-Group Discussion

1. What is one point in this book that challenged you and your perspective the most?

2. If you are active in ministry, in what ways would your ministry look different if you only had to focus on one person?
3. Why do you think more Christians do not commit to this kind of individualized ministry? What are they afraid of? What are their obstacles?
4. Share and discuss your "Discipleship Road Map" with the rest of the group.

Notes

1. Steve Shadrach, *The God Ask: A Fresh, Biblical Approach to Personal Support* (Fayetteville, AR: CMM Press, 2013).

2. Sherry Weddell, *Forming Intentional Disciples: The Path to Knowing and Following Jesus* (Huntington, IN: Our Sunday Visitor, 2012), 130.

3. Francis Chan, *Crazy Love: Overwhelmed by a Relentless God* (Colorado Springs, CO: David C. Cook, 2008), 112.

4. National Federation for Catholic Youth Ministry, "National Dialogue on Catholic Pastoral Ministry with Youth and Young Adults: Final Report," 2021, p. 78, https://www.nationaldialogue.info.

5. Pontifical Council for the Promotion of the New Evangelization, *Directory for Catechesis*, new ed. (Washington, DC: United States Conference of Catholic Bishops, 2020), 33b.

6. Weddell, *Forming Intentional Disciples*, 130.

Everett Fritz is founder and executive director of Andrew Ministries, a nonprofit devoted to training parishes in discipleship and family-based youth ministry. He has more than fifteen years of experience in youth ministry. He also is the author of *Freedom* and *The Art of Forming Young Disciples* and the coauthor of *Uncompromising Purity*.

Fritz has been a regular guest on EWTN, *Catholic Answers Live*, and numerous podcast and radio programs. He has spoken all across the country presenting on discipleship through missions, retreats, and workshops for dioceses, parishes, schools, and other organizations.

Fritz earned an associate's degree from Holy Cross College, a bachelor's degree in theology from Franciscan University of Steubenville, and a master's degree in theology with concentrations in catechesis and evangelization from the Augustine Institute.

He lives with his wife, Katrina, and their three children in Centennial, Colorado.

andrew-ministries.com
Facebook: Catholic Everett Fritz
Twitter: everettfritz
YouTube: Everett Fritz

Founded in 1865, Ave Maria Press, a ministry of the Congregation of Holy Cross, is a Catholic publishing company that serves the spiritual and formative needs of the Church and its schools, institutions, and ministers; Christian individuals and families; and others seeking spiritual nourishment.